Organizational Toxin Handlers

"Daniel provides an insightful discussion about how HR practitioners can act to protect employees from the constant barrage of toxic expectations commonly experienced within our organisations. The book highlights this unique role of HR practitioners as protectors and describes how they can shape their organisations to reduce the inherent toxicity. A book highly pertinent for HR practitioners, business students, and organisational scholars."

—Paula Brough, *Professor, School of Applied Psychology, Griffith University, Australia*

"We need to do what we can to eradicate toxic environments – this book gives clear insights into how to do this"

—Tony Wall, *Professor and Founder and Head, International Centre for Thriving at Work, University of Chester, UK*

Teresa A. Daniel

Organizational Toxin Handlers

The Critical Role of HR, OD, and Coaching Practitioners in Managing Toxic Workplace Situations

Foreword by Lynn Harrison

Teresa A. Daniel
Sullivan University
Louisville, KY, USA

Foreword by
Lynn Harrison
Black Tusk Leadership (BC) Inc
Vancouver, Canada

ISBN 978-3-030-51684-0   ISBN 978-3-030-51685-7 (eBook)
https://doi.org/10.1007/978-3-030-51685-7

© The Editor(s) (if applicable) and The Author(s), under exclusive licence to Springer Nature Switzerland AG 2020, corrected publication 2020

This work is subject to copyright. All rights are solely and exclusively licensed by the Publisher, whether the whole or part of the material is concerned, specifically the rights of translation, reprinting, reuse of illustrations, recitation, broadcasting, reproduction on microfilms or in any other physical way, and transmission or information storage and retrieval, electronic adaptation, computer software, or by similar or dissimilar methodology now known or hereafter developed.

The use of general descriptive names, registered names, trademarks, service marks, etc. in this publication does not imply, even in the absence of a specific statement, that such names are exempt from the relevant protective laws and regulations and therefore free for general use.

The publisher, the authors and the editors are safe to assume that the advice and information in this book are believed to be true and accurate at the date of publication. Neither the publisher nor the authors or the editors give a warranty, expressed or implied, with respect to the material contained herein or for any errors or omissions that may have been made. The publisher remains neutral with regard to jurisdictional claims in published maps and institutional affiliations.

This Palgrave Macmillan imprint is published by the registered company Springer Nature Switzerland AG.
The registered company address is: Gewerbestrasse 11, 6330 Cham, Switzerland

The author wishes to acknowledge the ground-breaking contributions of the late Peter J. Frost. Professor Frost was an expert in the field of organizational behavior who worked for many years at the University of British Columbia. His original identification of the term and his ideas about the important role of the organizational toxin handler (see, Frost, 2003, 2004, 2006; Frost & Robinson, 1999) served as the inspiration and foundation for both the author's initial empirical research study and also for this book—which is dedicated to his memory.

Foreword

As a former HR leader, organization development consultant, and executive coach, it is my honor to write the foreword of this very important book. The research that is at its foundation builds on the work of the late Peter Frost, who coined the term "toxic handler". Twenty years ago, Frost saw that those people in organizations who "voluntarily shoulder the sadness, frustration, bitterness and anger that are endemic to organizational life" were not only unsung heroes who performed a much needed function in the company, but individuals who, over time, often suffered from the weight of this emotionally intense work.

We need our toxin handlers more than ever today. Organizations are facing an accelerating pace of change, often *disruptive* change, upending familiar ways of doing things. Then there are mergers and acquisitions, downsizing, restructuring, increasing workloads, bullying bosses, and an unrelenting focus on outcomes, despite avowals that people are the number one asset. Beyond the growing demands at work, people are often struggling to deal with health concerns, aging parents, and childcare. As Daniel points out, the causes of stress in an organization are manifold, and sometimes chronic.

When toxin handlers help employees to get back on track or provide wise counsel to leaders who need to convey difficult messages, they help the organization to achieve its goals and purpose. They also save coworkers from a debilitating spiral of negativity and hopelessness. As Frost had noted, these kinds of painful emotions can be contagious, seeping like poison into the system, undetected. Unhealthy organizations do not attract or keep talented employees and they do not achieve great results.

Although toxin handlers can be anyone, the responsibility typically falls to the company's HR professionals, who provide behind-the-scenes support to both employees and managers. It is this group that Daniel's research addresses. Although HR practitioners naturally bring empathetic listening skills and a desire to solve problems, theirs is not always an easy task.

In the role of intermediary or systems support, HR leaders are often caught in the middle, trying to meet the needs of workers and managers who turn to them for guidance. In some cases, managers want HR to do their dirty work—convey unpleasant messages or clean up a poorly handled situation. And sometimes the best solution for the employee is not necessarily the best for the organization.

The pressures can mount as the HR professional responds to the various requests to provide emotional support and work with people to solve problems. Toxin handling is only part of their job, and is often not recognized for its importance, the time involved, and the toll it takes. One of the reasons for this is that it usually takes place behind closed doors and senior management often does not recognize or appreciate how much it is done.

Handling strong negative feelings, being regularly in the presence of troubled employees, and managing their own emotional toil is not something many HR practitioners have been trained for. As Daniel's research found, they are usually compassionate individuals who went into the field because they profoundly care about people. They feel good when they can help alleviate suffering in the workplace and develop creative solutions to problems that interfere with an employee's functioning. Sometimes these things are hard to achieve—or the amount of help that is needed is overwhelming. For the beleaguered HR professional, often feeling alone in their role or caught in the middle, the strain can be immense, leading to burnout or loss of spirit.

This book provides not only insight into the value of toxin handling, but also what is needed to support those who carry out this role in doing so in a way that is healthy. Some of the solutions are systemic—changes that organizations can make to acknowledge the need for this role and how to support those who provide it. Examples are including the toxin handling function in the HR job description, providing training and resources, rewarding this behavior, and enabling community support for the professional who engages in this emotionally taxing work. To prevent toxic behavior in the first place, the organization can screen prospective managers for their people skills, hold people accountable for civil and compassionate behavior, and invest in skills workshops in conflict resolution, communication, and emotional intelligence.

Daniel also offers suggestions, drawn from interviews with HR professionals, about how individuals can take care of themselves in order to take care of others. These include the need for physical and emotional fitness, positivity, paying attention to emotions and behaviors in oneself as well as others, coaching managers to take responsibility for employee relationships, setting boundaries, talking to a confidante, and meditation. Self-care can also include periodically taking a break from a stressful work environment.

This book comes at a crucial time in history. As the world faces an unprecedented pandemic, the need for toxin handling is greater than ever. Many people are frightened, for their own health, their family's wellbeing, for their jobs, and for their way of life. Organizations will need to revise not only the way they bring their products and services to market, but how employees work together. As we face this enormous challenge, Daniel's book reminds us of the critical importance of recognizing the all-too-human side of life in organizations. It also provides positive and practical steps to support those who rise to meet the emotional needs of employees, those HR professionals who continue to help people to thrive in life and in their jobs.

Black Tusk Leadership (BC) Inc Lynn Harrison
Vancouver, BC, Canada

Acknowledgments

The author wishes to express her sincere appreciation to Marcus Ballenger for believing in the concept of the book and for his encouragement and quick turnaround time at all stages of the project. He is a consummate professional and a delightful collaborator.

The author would also like to give a shout out to Chris Gray, a PhD student in management with a concentration in HR Leadership at Sullivan University. Gray is also an active HR Consultant with the United States Department of Veterans Affairs. He engaged in all stages of the empirical research study which serves as the foundation for this book. His contribution to the project went well beyond the typical role of a research assistant and his high-quality work is very much appreciated. I have every confidence that he will become an outstanding scholar-practitioner—and he is well on his way.

In addition, the author wishes to express her sincere appreciation to Sullivan University for the generous faculty grant which provided funding for the research project, as well as for their enthusiastic support and funding of her work over the years.

Finally, the author wishes to express her gratitude to the HR practitioners (who shall remain anonymous) who freely gave of their time to be interviewed for the research study which is foundational to this book. Both individually and as a group, they were articulate, thoughtful, smart, and impressive by any measure. Without them, this study would not have been possible and the American workplaces where they work would be far less humane.

Disclaimer

The author bears the sole responsibility for the content of this book, as well as for the underlying research study which serves as its foundation. The discussions and opinions contained herein do not necessarily reflect the views of her research assistant, Sullivan University, the study's participants, or the employees, officers, or directors of the Sullivan University System.

Contents

1 Toxin Handlers: Who They Are and What They Do — 1

2 What Causes Toxic Workplace Situations? A Focus on the Economic and Legal Drivers — 7

3 What Causes Toxic Workplace Situations? A Focus on the Individual, Situational, and Systemic Drivers — 17

4 What Causes Toxic Workplace Situations? A Focus on the Ethical Drivers — 37

5 Why They Do It — 45

6 How They Reduce Organizational Pain — 51

7 Why Organizations Need Them — 59

8 Friend or Assassin: Whose Side Is HR On, Anyway? — 63

9 The Price They Pay — 73

10 Running on Empty: Warning Signs of Compassion Fatigue and Burnout — 79

11	Perceived Low Value of HR's Work to Senior Leaders (and How HR Can Fix This)	89
12	Promising Macro Strategies to Minimize Harm to Toxin Handlers	101
13	Promising Micro Strategies to Minimize Harm to Toxin Handlers	113
14	Can We Reduce Organizational Toxicity by Improving Our Leaders? Hint: Yes, We Can!	119
15	The So-What? Making Sense of It All	129
16	Epilogue: A Manifesto for a New (and Better) Future	133

Correction to: The So-What? Making Sense of It All — C1

Appendix A: Executive Summary of the Research Study — 137

Appendix B: Technical Report — 141

Bibliography — 163

Index — 177

About the Author

Teresa A. Daniel, JD, PhD serves as dean and professor, Human Resource Leadership Programs at Sullivan University (www.sullivan.edu) based in Louisville, KY. She is also the chair for the HRL concentration in the university's PhD in Management program.

Daniel has a significant body of research in HR with an emphasis on two primary areas of inquiry: (1) *counterproductive work behaviors* (focused on workplace bullying, sexual harassment, and toxic leadership), and (2) *HR's unique role and its impact on organizational effectiveness* (e.g. in the management of toxic workplace emotions, responding to situations of workplace bullying and harassment, dealing with toxic leaders, and the management of people during mergers and acquisitions). Her research has been actively supported by the national Society for Human Resource Management (SHRM) through the publication of numerous articles and interviews, as well as by the publication of her book, co-authored with Gary Metcalf, titled *Stop Bullying at Work: Strategies and Tools for HR, Legal & Risk Management Professionals (2016)*.

Daniel was honored as an Initial Fellow of the *International Academy on Workplace Bullying, Mobbing, and Abuse* in 2014 and received the *Distinguished Alumnus Award* at Centre College in 2002. Most recently, she was the *2019 Grand Prize Winner* of the national SHRM HR Haiku contest.

HR makes it hum.

1

Toxin Handlers: Who They Are and What They Do

Layoffs, harassment, discrimination, mergers and acquisitions, personality conflicts, or an abusive boss are just a few of the many types of workplace situations that can generate intense emotional pain for employees—feelings like anger, frustration, stress, disappointment, and anxiety. For those required to report to work during the deadly #coronavirus outbreak, there is also now an element of abject fear that going to work may result in their own death or the demise of someone they love. With the lone exception of the pandemic, most of these workplace events are predictable—even somewhat inevitable. It is the way organizations handle them (or do not) that can create a serious problem for both employees and, ultimately, the organizations that they serve.

If these types of situations are managed poorly, the chronic anger or prolonged stress these situations create results in an undesirable by-product known as *organizational toxicity*. The word "toxic" comes from the Greek "toxikon" which means "arrow poison". In a literal sense, the term in its original form means to kill (poison) in a targeted way (arrow). Over time, the buildup of these toxic emotions will create a workplace culture where employees feel devalued, demoralized, and often hopeless—and most assuredly not productive or actively engaged.

Peter Frost (2003) first identified and coined the term for the special role some employees take on in an effort to alleviate this toxicity for employees—he referred to these individuals as *toxin handlers*. He described them as people within an organization who "voluntarily shoulder the sadness, frustration, bitterness, and the anger that are endemic to organizational life". Think of it this way: they act much like a kidney or the immune system in a human body—by neutralizing, dissipating, and dispersing organizational toxins that build up over time as a result of difficult decisions made by the organization, the consequences of which impact employees.

To get a better handle on this phenomenon and to see if HR practitioners could identify with it, we interviewed 26 highly educated and experienced HR professionals. What we found was really not that surprising—they reported that a central aspect of their role is to act as an *organizational toxin handler* (Daniel, 2018; *see also*, Daniel, 2017, 2019a, 2019b, 2019c). In fact, 58% of the study's participants said that they helped employees deal with toxic emotions on a *daily* basis (Daniel, 2018).

A high-level summary of this research, which is foundational to this book, is included as Appendix I should you wish to read more (Daniel, 2018). And for those of you who are more academically inclined or just wish to more closely examine how the results from the study were derived, a more comprehensive examination of the study's design and findings is included as Appendix II (Daniel, 2018).

You will see that quotes from the experienced HR professionals who were interviewed for this study are included throughout the following chapters to help explain key points. It is only fair to warn you at this point that hearing from practitioners—in their own words—may be painful and cause you to remember some of your own difficult workplace experiences. As tough (and sometimes poignant) as it may be to read them, their unvarnished perspectives are included because they help to underscore how organizational toxicity actually affects both the organization and its employees, including practitioners such as yourself.

This new label—*organizational toxin handler*—describes an old issue that most of you will quickly understand to be a persistent workplace problem for HR practitioners. In fact, you have likely personally experienced it at some point in your career and may even experience it multiple times per week. In all likelihood, you engage in these type of activities with some frequency but perhaps just didn't yet have a term or label with which to describe it. Now you do.

When engaged in this work, toxin handlers are involved in six core activities: empathetic listening, suggest solutions and provide resources, work behind the scenes and provide a safe space, confidential counseling, strategize communications and reframe difficult messages, and coach and advise managers. If you take a moment to reflect on what you do during a "normal" day, I would venture to guess that this is sounding like pretty familiar territory now, isn't it?

HR, OD, and coaching practitioners are regularly confronted by distressed employees and organizational leaders who bring emotionally charged problems to them with the expectation that they will receive help to resolve the issue. Any further reference to HR or HR practitioners is also meant to include OD and coaching practitioners since the nature of their work so closely aligns and frequently overlaps. For purposes of this book, though, I will generally refer to them collectively as "HR" or simply as "practitioners" for ease of reference.

By engaging in this work, organizational toxin handlers enable other employees to stay focused and do their jobs. Without them, the organizational toxicity would continue to build, resulting in higher levels of turnover, increased health costs, more litigation, and reduced levels of employee morale and productivity.

Toxin handlers care deeply about employees. They feel a strong need to listen to and assist employees in dealing with their problems, whether personal and organizational—they tend to think of themselves as inherently *fixers*.

Although toxin handlers routinely assist employees, at the same time they also feel a strong responsibility to support senior leaders and drive positive organizational outcomes. Navigating these competing role demands (which are often in direct conflict) is not easy. As a result, the role is inherently paradoxical and the nature of this required "balancing act" tends to create significant personal stress for practitioners.

Moreover, the toxin handling role is dangerous because of the personal risk it poses to the practitioner's personal well-being over time. They commonly experience significant physical and emotional exhaustion, feelings of sadness and anger, high stress, lack of sleep, and burnout. In addition, their personal relationships, overall health, and home life are also often negatively affected. This causes some to seek personal counseling and/or medical attention as a result of the excessive tension and strain they experience at work.

Pictures are often helpful in illuminating new concepts such as that of organizational toxin handler. To further accelerate your understanding of this role, here is a conceptual model which may help you to visualize the organizational role and how it impacts employee well-being and organizational effectiveness (Fig. 1.1).

The heart is a key element in visualizing and understanding the results of the study given that it demonstrates that HR practitioners are empathetic and compassionate listeners. The arrow to "Drives Career Choice" demonstrates that their empathetic and compassionate nature drives their career choice—becoming an HR professional. The arrow back to the heart demonstrates that it is this combination of empathy and compassion, in addition to the role itself, that works in tandem to drive employees to seek their counsel.

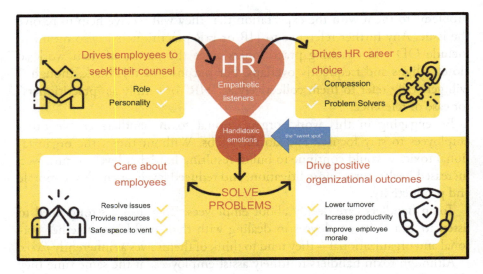

Fig. 1.1 Conceptual model of HR's role as organizational toxin handler (Daniel, 2018)

The "sweet spot" occurs when practitioners work to solve problems for both employees and their organization by being "HR fixers"—helping employees manage the toxic emotions that they feel as a result of workplace decisions and issues. They do this by providing care and concern for employees so that they feel understood and valued, while maintaining a sharp awareness of the need to keep their organizations functioning and profitable.

In the chapters that follow, we will delve further into the types of situations that create organizational toxicity, who toxin handlers are and what they actually *do*, how they do it, why organizations need them, and what companies can do to minimize the harm to their well-being resulting from the toxin handling role. The risks and dangers associated with the toxin handling role will also be examined, along with what practitioners themselves can do to protect themselves from the increased levels of stress, burnout, and emotional and physical exhaustion that they often experience due to their engagement in this important work. Stay with me to learn more about these topics—and more—in the coming chapters.

It may be useful to initially examine why toxic emotions are so prevalent at work to give you some context for the problem and how it has evolved over the past 30 years. As a result, we will next examine in Chap. 2 some of the economic and legal issues that have contributed to changes in the American workplace—changes that have increased the organizational toxicity that currently exists for so many employees.

References

Daniel, T. A. (2017, Winter). Managing toxic emotions at work: An examination of HR's unique role as the "organizational shock absorber". *Employment Relations Today, 43*(4), 13–19.

Daniel, T. A. (2018). *Managing toxic emotions at work: An empirical study of HR's role and its impact on personal well-being and organizational effectiveness.* https://doi.org/10.13140/RG.2.2.16315.26408.

Daniel, T. A. (2019a, March 6). Viewpoint: HR as toxin handlers. Society for Human Resource Management *HR News*. Retrieved from https://www.shrm.org/resourcesandtools/hr-topics/employee-relations/pages/are-you-a-toxin-handler.aspx.

Daniel, T. A. (2019b, March 13). Viewpoint: How HR can protect itself from toxic emotions. Society for Human Resource Management *HR News*. Retrieved from https://www.shrm.org/resourcesandtools/hr-topics/employee-relations/pages/viewpoint-how-hr-can-protect-itself-from-toxic-emotions.aspx.

Daniel, T. A. (2019c, March 25). Viewpoint: How toxin handlers reduce organizational pain. Society for Human Resource Management *HR News*. Retrieved from https://www.shrm.org/ResourcesAndTools/hr-topics/employee-relations/Pages/Viewpoint-How-Toxin-Handlers-Reduce-Organizational-Pain.aspx.

Frost, P. J. (2003). *Toxic emotions at work.* Boston: Harvard Business School Press.

2

What Causes Toxic Workplace Situations? A Focus on the Economic and Legal Drivers

Introduction

I suspect that many of you reading this book are all too familiar with situations in which you have to deal with the pain and emotion of employees caused by difficult workplace decisions or situations. Far too many American corporations are, to put it bluntly, in a state of chaos or disarray much of the time. Employees often come to work feeling overwhelmed, anxious, and sometimes bitter, and challenges related to the COVID-19 pandemic have made the situation even worse. Why? Because organizational leaders consciously (or unwittingly) make difficult decisions without communicating the rationale behind the decision or taking the time to help employees make sense of the changes. As a result, conditions that lead to creation of a toxic workplace are created and you—HR, OD, and coaching practitioners—are left to clean up the mess.

To be fair, many of the decisions that leaders are required to make are hard—really hard—like decisions to merge or acquire, downsize, return employees to the office during a global pandemic, or to sell or close operations altogether. Leaders are not all inherently evil or mean-spirited (although some most decidedly are). They are simply in positions that require them to make decisions that affect people and their livelihoods. They sometimes misuse their power and engage in uncivil tactics (e.g. bullying, ignoring, name-calling, and the like) which causes employees to experience varying levels of organizational toxicity.

Circumstances during the past three decades have resulted in an excessive emphasis on efficiency and productivity. When the pendulum swings too far in this direction, the natural tendency of for-profit corporations is to evolve toward sweatshops and monopolies. Assuming this is the current situation, a credible argument can be made that trying to civilize corporations is much like trying to turn tigers into vegetarians. They will always be wild beasts by nature unless we "tame" them by changing our attitudes and expectations (and laws) about what is proper conduct in the workplace when it comes to the management of people. Some of the historical context which has fueled the growth of toxicity in the American workplace over the last 30 years will be examined next.

How We Got Here: Some Historical Background

A Relentless Focus on the Maximization of Profits

Many years ago, Milton Friedman wrote a highly influential *New York Times* essay in which he contended that "the (only) responsibility of business is to maximize profits" (Friedman, 1970). With limited exceptions, there has been widespread acceptance of his view since that time. Corporations obviously need to achieve results and be profitable, but that is only *part* of their responsibility. They also are responsible for maximizing all of their assets, including people. As noted by Kenneth Mason, quoted in Makower (2006):

> The moral imperative all of us share in this world is that of getting the best return we can on whatever assets we are privileged to employ. What American business leaders too often forget is that this means all the assets employed—not just the financial assets but also the brains employed, the labor employed, the materials employed, and the land, air, and water employed. (p. 31)

Fueled by activist shareholders, private-equity firms, and bonuses based on stock prices, it seems that corporate leaders instead have become obsessed with maximizing quarterly profits—and they have been quite successful in doing so. In fact, the stock market has just recently hit all-time record highs in recent years (Thorbecke, 2020). Ironically, though, as corporate and investor profits continue to climb, real wages for American workers have barely budged in terms of their actual buying power (Gould, 2018).

Institutional investors have had great influence on corporate decision-making in recent years. They seem to believe that caring about anything except profits is inappropriate, and even possibly a violation of management's fiduciary responsibility (Greider, 2003). As a result of this short-term focus, many companies fail to adequately consider the interests of their other key stakeholders: customers, employees, and society. The result is a de-humanizing of the American workplace. It has become a place where people are often treated badly and managers are rewarded for engaging in those very behaviors. As noted by Edwards (1996):

> The forbidden truth is that we are living by a set of lies which are necessary for short-term profit, at the expense of human physical and psychological life and global environmental integrity. We are living in a system where power ensures that the requirements of profit take priority over the requirements of living things […]. Consequently, our freedom extends as far as, and no further than, the satisfaction of these requirements, with all else being declared neurosis, paranoia, communism, extremism, the work of the devil, or Neptunian nonsense. (p. 163)

This profit obsession has created significant changes for employees working in American corporations over the last 30 years. It is these changes that will be examined next.

Changes in the American Workplace

In the past, working for a corporation was significantly defined by promises. Corporations committed to provide employees with lifetime job security, fair compensation, health care, and a secure retirement plan. In exchange, employees promised to show up every day to perform their work while being loyal to the organization. Together, this unspoken understanding between employers and employees formed the implicit "social contract" of the work relationship (Kochan & Shulman, 2007).

This relationship often caused employees to feel like children—the company was the "parent" (e.g. giving direction as well as an allowance, while also providing security) and the employee was the "dutiful child" (e.g. following orders and not questioning authority in exchange for the protections and benefits offered by the organization). Though employees were often frustrated with the repetition of their jobs and the autocratic nature of their supervisors, these corporate promises were generally enough to justify the trade-offs.

The essential nature of this parent-child relationship remains in place at most organizations even today. While some companies have worked hard to develop cultures where employees are treated very well, others follow a more ruthless and domineering approach. Just like the actual parent-child relationship which exists at home, unless laws are directly and egregiously broken, there are no binding rules of behavior which require leaders to be kind to employees, or even civil.

This relationship developed as a result of the focus by organizations on efficiency. In large-scale operations, it was generally less expensive to purchase labor in bulk than to hire craftsmen by the hour to perform each task. For workers, this meant selling control over their time, energy, and talents to someone else. For corporations, the problem was utilization. Paying for 40 hours of labor if only 30 were needed was wasteful. The common understanding was (and still is) that all *means of production*—both human and technical—should be utilized to their fullest extent. Dealing with machines was less complex; they only had to be fueled and maintained. The humans, however, had to be *managed*; someone had to divide and coordinate the work, and to watch over the employees in order to make sure that they were productive and efficient.

Labor unions were then created to protect the rights of workers. As jobs were progressively automated, more educated workers were needed to meet the requirements of higher-skilled roles. Largely due to legislation, working conditions improved in terms of safety and health. While the legal definitions and fundamental nature of corporations remained intact and unchanged, the nature of the employment relationship did not (Greider, 2003, 2009).

Over time, who works, how work is carried out, and the conditions of employment have changed dramatically, but the public and organizational policies and practices governing work and the employment relationship (originally put in place in the 1930s to fit the industrial economy and workforce of that time) have not kept pace. The social contract that governed work and the trust that it engendered for many years is now long gone, and those historical promises have been irretrievably broken (Kochan & Shulman, 2007; Greider, 2003).

Employees have witnessed—either personally or through the experience of their parents or grandparents—massive job cuts, significant reductions in or elimination of employee benefit plans and policy benefits and increasing health care costs being passed along to employees. They have also seen pension plans, along with medical benefits, eliminated or drastically reduced because of a failing economy and escalating costs.

Worse yet, they have witnessed the painful aftermath of decisions made to eliminate or reduce retiree benefits under those plans—long after employees actually retired and left the workplace based on those sacred commitments. It is no surprise, then, that so many young employees are highly pessimistic about work and the economy. They are also reluctant to commit to employment in the corporate sector; as a result, roughly one-third of young adults are uninsured and that figure is rising (McCarthy, 2019).

Since organizations are no longer committed to the future of their workers (either in terms of providing job security or providing for their retirement), employees frequently adopt a "me first" strategy of self-preservation. This has resulted in "job hopping" and a lack of loyalty or long-term commitment by employees to their organizations.

While the "parent-child" analogy remains true, the current employment relationship can also be described as that of "master-servant" given the imbalance of power and distinct hierarchies that exist in most organizations (Greider, 2003). Employees working for an organization are governed by different rights, privileges, and legal protections than the general public. In essence, employees lose their "personhood" when they go to work. As Levering (1988) observed:

> We generally accept as a given the contrast between our time at work and the rest of our lives. Once you enter the office or factory, you lose many of the rights you enjoy as a citizen. There's no process for challenging—or changing—bad decisions made by the authorities. There's no mechanism to vote for people to represent you in decision-making bodies … We take for granted that such rights and protections don't apply to the workplace, partly because most of us have never seen examples to the contrary. (p. 62)

Greider (2003) further confirmed this societal disconnect when he described the grim reality of work in modern America:

> In pursuit of "earning a living" most Americans go to work for someone else and thereby accept the employer's right to command their behavior in intimate detail. At the factory gate or the front office, people implicitly forfeit claims to self-direction and are typically barred from participating in the important decisions that govern their daily efforts. Most employees lose any voice in how the rewards of the enterprise are distributed, the surplus wealth their own work helped to create. Basic rights the founders said were inalienable—free speech and freedom of assembly, among others—are effectively suspended, consigned to the control of others. In some ways, the employee also surrenders essential elements of self (p. 49).

The general legal status of employees in the United States reinforces the model of unilateral management control. The predominant rule of "at will" employment—the right of an employer to terminate an employee for any reason or for no reason at all—contributes significantly to this uneven power dynamic (Greider, 2003; Summers, 2000). Perversely, a boss who screams at a subordinate is deemed to be exercising "management prerogative", while the subordinate who responds by yelling back or even asking for an apology can be fired on the spot (Yamada, 2013b). As a result, employees "can be fired for doing what's right—making a moral choice—and they frequently are" (Greider, 2003, p. 78).

When individuals enter the workplace, they do not (and should not) abdicate their right to be treated fairly and humanely. At a bare minimum, most would agree that employers should be required to observe workplace norms for mutual respect. As Hornstein (1996) noted:

> No matter what the circumstances, bosses may not abuse others. They may not lie, restrict, or dictate employees' behavior outside the workplace, threaten harm, or protect themselves at the expense of those more vulnerable. Positions of greater power in organizations' hierarchy do not grant license to show favoritism, humiliate or behave as masters or gods. (p. 143)

For more than three decades now, management experts, scholars, practitioners, and authors of popular business books have urged American employers to treat their employees with respect and dignity. Recommendations to-date have placed a heavy emphasis on the need for strong leadership, fair employment policies, comprehensive benefit programs, grievance processes, and frequent communication. In addition, organizations have been urged to emphasize ethics, integrity, and fair dealing in the conduct of their business for many years. *See*, for example Andersson & Pearson, 1999; Daniel & Metcalf, 2001, 2016; Daniel, 2003a, 2003b, 2006, 2009a, 2009b, 2009c, 2012a, 2012b, 2013; Deming, 2000; Drucker, 1992; Goldsmith et al., 2003; Hartling & Sparks, 2002; Hornstein, 1996, 2003; Levering, 1988; Namie & Namie, 2000, 2003, 2009; Miller, 1986; Peters & Waterman, 1982; Sutton, 2007; and Yamada, 2008, 2013a, 2013b, to name but a few.

Despite these vigorous efforts to promote the development of a more humane and respectful workplace, progress has been frustratingly slow. The idea that an individual is entitled to be treated with dignity at work, sadly, remains a "somewhat revolutionary concept" (Yamada, 2008, p. 56). Recent history confirms that workers' rights have only increased, for the most part, when laws and regulations have been imposed on corporations (Greider, 2003; Yamada, 2008). The rights of workers to bargain through unions, equal employment laws (including anti-discrimination measures), and laws protecting employees against sexual harassment are simply recent social attempts to civilize the corporate workplace. Given the perniciousness and continued frequency of many of these issues, it is not difficult to conclude that organizational toxicity will continue to reign supreme in American corporations, but I remain a persistent optimist.

The reasons that I am hopeful? Because it appears that the status quo may be shattering due to the revolutionary impact of the #coronavirus pandemic to the ways we both work and live (Solnit, 2020). Some of the more hopeful changes taking place include more employees than ever now working from home, increased recognition of the need for everyone to have health care coverage, more scheduling flexibility, increased awareness of an employee's family responsibilities, and increasing trust among employers that employees will actually do their jobs even when they are not under the watchful eyes of supervisors at the office.

Many things we once thought were impossible—like significant extensions to worker's rights and benefits—have happened virtually overnight as a result of the pandemic (Solnit, 2020). Economic assistance in the form of $1200 checks to most Americans, paid sick leave and expanded family and medical leave mandates, and enhanced unemployment benefits are just some of the positive changes that have recently come to pass (e.g. *Families First Coronavirus Response Act*, 2020; *Coronavirus Aid, Relief, and Economic Security Act*, 2020, among others). We can only hope that these proactive and positive changes will create a profound and lasting shift that continues to help humanize our workplaces—and that the changes remain in place long after the virus has left us.

References

Andersson, L. M., & Pearson, C. M. (1999). Tit for tat? The spiraling effect of incivility in the workplace. *Academy of Management Review, 24*, 452–471.

Coronavirus Aid, Relief, and Economic Security Act. (2020). Retrieved from https://home.treasury.gov/policy-issues/cares.

Daniel, T. A. (2003a). Tools for building a positive employee relations environment. *Employment Relations Today, 30*(2), 51–64. Retrieved from http://onlinelibrary.wiley.com/doi/10.1002/ert.10086/abstract

Daniel, T. A. (2003b). Developing a "culture of compliance" to prevent sexual harassment. *Employment Relations Today, 30*(3), 33–42. Retrieved from http://onlinelibrary.wiley.com/doi/10.1002/ert.10096/abstract

Daniel, T. A. (2006). Bullies in the workplace: A focus on the "abusive disrespect" of employees. *SHRM Whitepapers*. Retrieved from http://moss07.shrm.org/Research/Articles/Articles/Pages/CMS_018341.aspx.

Daniel, T. A. (2009a). *"Tough boss" or workplace bully: A grounded theory study of insights from human resource professionals.* Doctoral dissertation, Fielding Graduate University. Retrieved from http://gradworks.umi.com/33/50/3350585.html.

Daniel, T. A. (2009b). *Stop bullying at work: Strategies and tools for HR & legal professionals.* Alexandria, VA: SHRM Books. Retrieved from http://shrmstore.shrm.org

Daniel, T. A. (2009c, July 12–17). *Workplace bullying in American organizations: The path from recognition to prohibition.* 53rd Annual Conference of the International Society for the Systems Sciences, The University of Queensland, Brisbane. Retrieved from http://journals.isss.org/index.php/proceedings53rd/article/viewFile/1209/400.

Daniel, T. A. (2012a, June 13–15). *HR in the crossfire: An exploration into the role of HR and workplace bullying.* 8th International Conference on Workplace Bullying and Harassment, University of Copenhagen, Copenhagen, Denmark. Retrieved from http://bullying2012.com/programme/DETAILED_CONFERENCE_PROGRAMME_version_12.pdf/.

Daniel, T. A. (2012b, Spring). Caught in the crossfire: When HR practitioners become targets of bullying. *Employment Relations Today, 39*(1), 9–16. Retrieved from http://onlinelibrary.wiley.com/doi/10.1002/ert.21349/abstract.

Daniel, T. A. (2013, Summer). Executive success and the increased potential for ethical failure. *SHRM Legal Report.* Alexandria, VA: SHRM. Retrieved from http://www.shrm.org/publications/pages/default.aspx.

Daniel, T. A., & Metcalf, G. S. (2001). *The management of people in mergers & acquisitions.* Westport, CT: Quorum Books. Retrieved from http://www.amazon.com/The-Management-People-Mergers-Acquisitions/dp/1567203698

Daniel, T. A., & Metcalf, G. S. (2016). *Stop bullying at work: Strategies and tools for HR, legal & risk management professionals.* Alexandria, VA: SHRM Books.

Deming, W. E. (2000). *The new economics for industry, government, education* (2nd ed.). Cambridge: MIT Press.

Drucker, P. F. (1992). *Managing for the future: The 1990's and beyond.* New York: Penguin Group.

Edwards, D. (1996). *Burning all illusions: A guide to personal and political freedom.* Cambridge, MA: South End Press.

Families First Coronavirus Response Act. (2020). Retrieved from https://www.dol.gov/agencies/whd/pandemic/ffcra-employer-paid-leave.

Friedman, M. (1970, September 13). The social responsibility of business is to increase its profits. *The New York Times Magazine.* Retrieved from http://www.colorado.edu/studentgroups/libertarians/issues/friedman-soc-resp-business.html.

Goldsmith, M., et al. (2003). *Global leadership: The next generation.* Upper Saddle River, NJ: Pearson Education, Inc.

Gould, E. (2018). *State of working America wages 2018.* Retrieved from https://www.epi.org/publication/state-of-american-wages-2018/.

Greider, W. (2003). *The soul of capitalism: Opening paths to a moral economy.* New York: Simon & Schuster.

Greider, W. (2009, May 6). The future of the American dream. *The Nation*. Retrieved from http://www.thenation.com/article/future-american-dream.

Hartling, L., & Sparks, E. (2002). *Relational-cultural practice: Working in a non-relational world*. No. 97. Wellesley, MA: Stone Center Working Papers Series.

Hornstein, H. A. (1996). *Brutal bosses and their prey: How to identify and overcome abuse in the workplace*. New York: Riverhead Books.

Hornstein, H. A. (2003, November/December). Workplace incivility: An unavoidable product of human nature and organizational nurturing. *Ivey Business Journal, 68*, 1–7.

Kochan, T., & Shulman, B. (2007, February 22). A new social contract: Restoring dignity and balance to the economy. *Briefing Paper #184*. Retrieved from www.epi.org.

Levering, R. (1988). *A great place to work: What makes some employers so good-and most so bad*. New York: Random House.

Makower, J. (2006, November 24). *Milton Friedman and the social responsibility of business*. Retrieved from http://www.greenbiz.com/news/2006/11/24/milton-friedman-and-social-responsibility-business.

McCarthy, N. (2019, September 18). The number of uninsured Americans is rising again—And young adults are most likely to lack coverage. *Forbes*. Retrieved from https://www.forbes.com/sites/niallmccarthy/2019/09/18/the-number-of-uninsured-americans-is-rising-again%2D%2Dand-young-adults-who-are-most-likely-to-lack-coverage/#2fc251795b62.

Miller, J. B. (1986). *What do we mean by relationships?* The Stone Center for Development Services & Studies at Wellesley College Colloquium, 1(2).

Namie, G., & Namie, R. F. (2000, 2003, 2009). *The bully at work: What you can do to stop the hurt and reclaim your dignity on the job*. Naperville, IL: Sourcebooks.

Peters, T. J., & Waterman, R. H. (1982). *In search of excellence: Lessons from America's best-run companies*. New York: Harper Collins.

Solnit, R. (2020, April 7). The impossible has already happened: What coronavirus can teach us about hope. *The Guardian*. Retrieved from https://www.theguardian.com/world/2020/apr/07/what-coronavirus-can-teach-us-about-hope-rebecca-solnit.

Summers, C. W. (2000). Employment at will in the United States: The divine right of employers. *Journal of Labor & Employment Law, 3*(65), 67–68.

Sutton, R. I. (2007). *The no asshole rule: Building a civilized workplace and surviving one that isn't*. New York: Warner Business Books.

Thorbecke, C. (2020, January 10). The Dow Jones reaches 29,000 for the 1st time in history. *ABC News*. Retrieved from https://abcnews.go.com/Business/dow-jones-broke-29000-1st-time-history/story?id=68195223.

Yamada, D. C. (2008). Workplace bullying and ethical leadership. *Journal of Values-Based Leadership, 1*(2). Retrieved from http://papers.ssrn.com/sol3/papers.cfm?abstract_id=1301554

Yamada, D. C. (2013a, March 1). Emerging American legal responses to workplace bullying. *Temple Political & Civil Rights Law Review, 22.* Suffolk University Law School Research Paper No. 13-7. Retrieved from http://ssrn.com/abstract=2242945.

Yamada, D. C. (2013b, April 1). Words rarely heard: 'Boss, I think you need to get some help'. *Minding the Workplace Blog.* Retrieved from http://newworkplace.wordpress.com/2013/04/page/2/.

3

What Causes Toxic Workplace Situations? A Focus on the Individual, Situational, and Systemic Drivers

An Examination of Workplace Dynamics

Although some will undoubtedly disagree, it is my contention that American corporations unwittingly create environments where the creation of toxic emotions and organizational toxicity is a conscious choice, despite the negative fallout to employees. In most corporate settings, there is a relentless pressure to achieve financial results; however, there are typically no rewards or recognition for being a "nice guy" who treats employees with kindness, compassion, or empathy. The idea that "what gets measured gets done" tends to pervade organizational life—and what gets measured are goals related to efficiency, productivity, and profitability.

My assertion is *not* that private workplace settings conspire to turn good people into monsters. To the contrary, many people around the world have long-term friendships which began in the workplace, while others find great personal satisfaction as a result of their work (I met the love of my life at work and he became my husband and frequent collaborator, so there's that angle too). Still others feel both deeply valued and respected by their colleagues, giving them a sense of validation and purpose. The point is that these are not *necessary conditions* of the workplace.

In this chapter, the dynamics presently occurring in the workplace will be explored from three perspectives: (1) *individual drivers*—the unique characteristics of the individuals involved, (2) *situational drivers*—the influence of the corporate situational context, and (3) *systemic drivers*—a view which poses larger questions about the nature of the social systems within which we work.

The individual characteristics of successful leaders will be examined first in an effort to explain why some individuals decide to use abusive tactics at work which generate organizational toxicity.

The Individual Perspective

A Focus on Results—Not How They Are Obtained

In my experience (and likely yours too), organizational leaders are typically intense and highly-driven individuals. Though they are often very effective, their forceful personalities and passion to meet and exceed goals can cause great distress to employees. Organizations with a culture focused on results at any cost create a situation where individuals with certain personalities seem to thrive. Due to their social competence and political skills, some high-performance leaders are also able to strategically abuse co-workers and yet continue to be evaluated positively by their supervisors (Treadway, Shaughnessy, Breland, Yang, & Reeves, 2013).

Levinson (1978) uses the term *abrasive personality* to describe executives who exhibit competitive, dominating, and controlling tendencies that create friction in interpersonal relationships (p. 86). In his view, such individuals seem to operate as though they were somehow privileged and "as if [they] had the right to be different or even inconsiderate" (p. 88). Levinson generously excuses their irritating and alienating behaviors as attributes of their need for perfection.

Kaplan (1991) uses the term *expansive executive* to describe a similar kind of leader who over-relies on accomplishment (p. 5). Like the manager with an abrasive personality, expansive executives are intense, driven, and unaware of their impact on others. Many are valued contributors who consistently produce outstanding results but harm the organization in the process. As he notes: "These executives reduce the organization's talent pool by driving people away and demoralizing those who remain" (p. 111).

Kramer (2006) refers to leaders who rule through intimidation and fear at work as *great intimidators*. In his view, these are individuals who "seem to relish the chaos they create because, in their minds, it's constructive. Time is short, the stakes are high, and the measures required are draconian". Great intimidators are "rough, loud, and in your face", they have the political intelligence necessary to get the job done, and they are willing to strategically utilize fear and anxiety to do so.

Ludeman and Erlandson (2006) describe these leaders as being people who have a propensity for what they refer to as *alpha risks*. Included in this category are characteristics of hard-driving competitiveness, interpersonal impatience, and a difficulty controlling anger (p. 17). Although not all alpha managers are male, many are. Like the abrasive personality and the expansive executive, the alpha male suffers from a lack of awareness about his impact on others, but clearly causes them distress. In the foreword of Ludeman and Erlandson's (2006) book, Marshall Goldsmith wrote:

> Many alpha males are designated at a very young age as high-potential leaders. This anointment can quickly degenerate into the "golden boy" syndrome, in which they believe that they are endowed with godlike qualities and have no need to ever change. As they advance through their careers, puffed up by their achievements, they often fail to see the interpersonal de-railers that are obvious to the rest of the world—and that will ultimately lead to their downfall. (p. ix)

Daniel (2009) found a clear distinction between "tough bosses" and those who cross the line to become workplace bullies. One of the primary differences was the presence of *malice* in the actions of bullies, defined as "the desire to cause pain, injury, or distress to another" (p. 156). While tough bosses are intensely results-oriented and not necessarily easy to work for, they are perceived by their employees to be fair-minded and professional—their focus is on achieving results for the organization. On the other hand, workplace bullies are more concerned with advancing their own personal agenda and are perceived as unfair and often out of control.

Why They Do It

These studies beg further questions about the individual characteristics of abusive leaders. If their actions go beyond what is actually functional for the organization and there are signs of pain, injury, or distress to another person, why would the leader continue to engage in such negative behavior?

One hypothesis suggests that leaders who exhibit highly aggressive characteristics are narcissistic (self-obsessed), sociopathic (lacking social conscience), or even psychopathic (lacking basic empathy) (Schouten & Silver, 2012; Boddy, 2011; Babiak & Hare, 2006; Hare, 1993). Peck (1998) uses the term "evil personality" to explain why some individuals use their power "to destroy the spiritual growth of others for the purpose of defending and preserving the integrity of their own sick selves" (p. 119).

Similarly, Lubit (2004) point to the personal deficiency of the leader and argues that they are, in fact, disturbed individuals who are power-hungry, enjoy hurting innocent people, and lack normal inhibitions and empathy. He suggests that their central aim is simply to intimidate and hurt others (p. 117). Hornstein (1996, p. 50) and Horn (2002) both posit that these toxic behaviors have little to do with general work-related stress but are a result of an abuse of power that is "knowing and deliberate".

Others focus less on individual deficiencies and explain that the behavior is due mostly to lack of awareness. These researchers argue that many people simply do not see the distress they are causing, and are generally receptive to a different way of managing after they undergo coaching or counseling (Crawshaw, 2005, 2007; Levinson, 1978; Livingston, 2001; Kaplan, 1991; Ludeman & Erlandson, 2006). Ultimately, though, it is undisputed that something drives aggression in these individuals beyond the point of generally acceptable social norms.

The success of the "results at all costs" strategy was recently confirmed by a study in which researchers determined that aggressive leaders who are abusive to others are more likely to enjoy professional success than even their more competent rivals (Cheng, Tracy, Foulsham, Kingstone, & Henrick, 2013). Why? Because people are impressed by their dominance. While not universally liked, the most dominant individuals were *feared* which led to an increase in their social standing and resulting organizational success. This two-part study looked at how "dominance" (defined as the use of force and intimidation to induce fear) and "prestige" (defined in the study as the appearance of skill and competency) can be used to achieve social rank and influence.

The researchers found that those rated as more dominant and prestigious were also rated as more influential. Ironically, while participants preferred leaders with prestige, they were actually more likely to choose dominant leaders. They also tended to be more forgiving of their bad behavior. These results might help to explain the prevalence and high rate of success among aggressive leaders in business. As noted by Furnham (2009):

> The business world often calls for (and rewards) arrogant, self-confident and self-important people. But, as anyone who works with and for them knows, they can destabilize and destroy working groups by their deeply inconsiderate behavior (p. 212).

Through a relentless focus on results at any cost and no consequences for the use of overly aggressive tactics to achieve them, our corporations inadvertently encourage bad behavior that creates organizational toxicity for employees. As Ford (2005) noted:

> In the real world, bullies are often the winners. They are the so-called tough bosses who have pushed their way to the top over the heads of their weaker and less aggressive colleagues. They are an archetype. They are the bulldogs, the pit bulls, the take-charge guys. They are the Donald Trump's of our lives.
>
> In the business world, bullies are rewarded. They are lionized. They are imitated and toadied to. Too often, the men and women who report to them adopt the same attitude toward the people they supervise, and so it goes down the line until you have a toxic work environment. Little wonder schools are incapable of routing bullies; the world around them can't and won't. (p. 138)

There seems to be a disconnect about what companies claim to want from leaders and the types of behavior they actually reward. What tends to be perceived as simply "strong management" in the office would normally be seen as confrontational and out-of-line outside of the workplace. This type of behavior is rewarded because management turns a blind eye to the process—the *way*—by which the results are actually obtained.

All too often, individuals are rewarded solely for achieving their goals, despite the destruction and demoralization of people along the way. Leaders who essentially operate without regard for others often successfully navigate the social and political organizational environment and achieve high ratings of performance, suggesting that there is a functional perspective associated with the use of bad behavior (Treadway et al., 2013).

We Idolize Arrogance and Outliers

While there is general consensus that the behavior of abusive leaders is unacceptable, for some reason they continue to command our interest and attention. There is something about the phenomenon that is either so provocative or so repulsive (or maybe both), that we sometimes inadvertently seem to support it by our failure to intervene (Nunberg, 2012a, 2012b). Some have referred to this fascination with those who operate outside the rules as the "charisma of villainy" (DiSalvo, 2012).

Regardless of the reasons, though, people who work outside of the accepted norms attract and hold our interest—at either extreme. One can be both a genius and a jerk (think Steve Jobs) or just a jerk. These outliers do not follow the accepted corporate rules and accepted norms; instead, they strategically use them to suit their own personal purposes and usually for their own personal gain (Rogers, 2011).

Psychological research over the past few years is beginning to reveal why this is so. Anderson, Brion, Moore, and Kennedy (2012) examined whether there is any adaptive advantage created by overconfidence at work, especially given that the trait so often leads to errors. The short answer is that even if overconfidence produces sub-par results, others still perceive it positively. In other words, overconfident people are perceived as having more social status, and social status in the corporate world is golden.

Another study highlights a similar result, but this time with respect to rudeness. Being rude is a categorically negative behavior by most standards; however, research suggests that we also see it as a sign of power. A study by Van Kleef, Homan, Finkenauer, Gundemir, and Stamkon (2011) found that the ruder someone acts, the more convinced observers become that he or she is powerful, and therefore does not have to respect normal rules. Powerful people smile less, interrupt others, and speak in a louder voice. When people do not respect the basic rules of social behavior, they lead others to believe that they have power, even if the observers would otherwise judge those violations as rude or flatly wrong.

Considering the many arrogant people in business and politics that our society seems to venerate, these findings actually make a lot of sense. Perhaps it is not the rudeness and corruption we admire, but more that the organization allows them to get away with it that intrigues us. It is this situational perspective—the organizational structure and context that appear to encourage (or at least support) abusive behavior—that will be examined next.

The Situational Perspective

Low Perceived Risk and No Consequences

Bad behavior often occurs when the perpetrator assesses the costs of engaging in those behaviors as being relatively small. The costs involve the risk of getting a reprimand or being fired, while the benefits can be higher pay, bonuses, promotions, and increasing levels of power and influence. The importance of perceived low costs and low risks can be illustrated by the fact that abusive conduct is more frequent in large (Einarsen, Raknes, & Matthiesen, 1994; Leymann, 1990) and bureaucratic organizations (Thylefors, 1987). Einarsen, Schanke, Aasland, and Skogstad (2007) have pointed out that the length and formality of an organization's decision-making processes make the individual less visible, thus reducing the risks to the perpetrator of being reprimanded.

In addition, there seems to be an association between abusive behavior and leadership style. A laissez-faire style of leadership or "weak" or "inadequate" leadership at higher organizational levels seems to be conducive to the use of abusive tactics (Einarsen et al., 1994; Hoel & Cooper, 2000; Leymann, 1996). The failings of this type of leadership style have been understood since the social climate studies of Lewin, Lippitt, and White (1939); however, those early lessons seem to have been forgotten. It is reasonable to assume that weak leaders will seldom intervene or respond to reports of abusive behaviors; similarly, it is reasonable to assume that the risk of discipline or other consequences is also low. As a result, it becomes a useful strategy when it can be reasonably expected that leaders will not do anything to stop it.

Organizational culture also has an impact on the prevalence of bad behavior in an organization. Brodsky (1976, p. 83) stated that "for harassment to occur, harassment elements must exist within a culture that permits and rewards harassment". If there is no policy against abusive tactics, no monitoring, or no punishment, a reasonable interpretation is that the organization simply accepts it as a legitimate leadership style. When this is the case, a possible perpetrator will then perceive the costs and dangers of engaging in such actions as very low.

A focus on excellence may also contribute to an acceptance of abusive conduct. For example, the abusive behavior of some top chefs can partly be attributed to their relentless pursuit of perfection (Johns & Menzel, 1999). Similarly, some companies and organizational cultures may even celebrate leaders who appear to be "hard-charging, tough guys" (Neuman & Baron, 2011).

Modeling and imitation may also influence its prevalence (O'Leary-Kelly, Griffin, & Glew, 1996). When new managers are socialized into a culture that treats abusive interactions as a "normal and acceptable way of getting things done", the problem increases (Hearn & Parkin, 2001). Social learning theory suggests that individuals who operate in a work environment where others are rewarded for aggressive behavior are more likely to engage in similar acts themselves (Bandura, 1973).

Abusive conduct can also be an initiation ritual, much like fraternity or sorority hazing. The fact that many victims consider complaining about abuse to be an act of organizational disloyalty further emphasizes the potential strength and impact of the socialization process (Hoel & Salin, 2003). Further, Pearson and Porath (2009) argue that with increasing informality and casual behavior in organizations, it may be more difficult for some employees to distinguish what constitutes "proper" and "professional" interpersonal behavior. Perceived hostility and injustice can also start escalating processes and a desire to reciprocate, thereby resulting in spirals of incivility or aggression (Andersson & Pearson, 1999).

Some organizational cultures are characterized by a heavy reliance on jokes and banter. For example, in typically male-dominated manufacturing environments, humiliating jokes and "funny surprises" can be an accepted part of the culture (Collinson, 1988; Einarsen & Raknes, 1997); however, this kind of humor can easily go bad, inadvertently creating a toxic work environment.

The bottom line of all of these studies: abusive leaders see no reason *not* to use aggressive and abusive tactics because there are generally no consequences for doing so; at the same time, the potential rewards can be quite significant. It is the potential payoffs of using an abusive strategy that will be discussed next.

Competition for Promotions, Influence, and Rewards Encourages Bullying

Though perhaps unintended, there are actually a lot of good reasons that a person might choose to use abusive tactics at work. Zapf and Einarsen (2011) point out that as individuals strive to be promoted, have influence, and acquire resources (p. 185)—what they refer to as *micro-political behavior*—it is not surprising that they would use competitive behaviors to get ahead. In fact, these behaviors might be the most "rational" of all forms of workplace aggression given that seeking to be successful through the achievement of promotions, rewards, and/or influence are generally accepted as "reasonable" workplace motives (Treadway et al., 2013; Salin, 2003).

Similarly, other researchers have also argued that abusive conduct is not actually an irrational behavior. Kräkel (1997) has suggested that it can sometimes be explained as "rent-seeking behavior"—that is, behavior that is intended to increase an individual's pay or bonuses. A study conducted by Cornell University's Center for Advanced Human Resource Studies (2012) confirmed this point of view. They found that disagreeable men earn an average of 18% more than their more agreeable colleagues. Interestingly, women did not receive the same pay bump for being less agreeable. Thus, if there is low perceived cost, and the perpetrator feels that he may actually benefit from using abusive tactics (e.g. by receiving higher pay or bonuses), this type of conduct quickly becomes a rational alternative.

There are several other instances where it might be individually rational or rewarding to terrorize a colleague or a subordinate. High internal competition and a politicized climate seem to make an organization particularly prone to misconduct (Sperry, 2009; O'Moore, 2000; Salin, 2003). In addition, the reward system may contribute to the problem. If an organization promotes an employee who has succeeded by manipulating or harming a colleague, it is inadvertently condoning the behavior and providing an incentive for others to do the same (O'Leary-Kelly et al., 1996).

Moreover, when pay or bonuses are based on a relative ranking of employees (Kräkel, 1997), an individual may be more motivated to abuse colleagues and subordinates. In fact, by sabotaging the work of a colleague, the perpetrator may improve his or her own standing (Treadway et al., 2013). In addition, if an employee is evaluated based on the performance of the team to which he belongs, he may want to expel very low performing team members who could negatively impact his pay or bonus. In this respect, teamwork can sometimes lead to oppressive control from peers (Sewell & Wilkinson, 1992).

Similarly, insults (which often play on hidden desires or vulnerabilities) can be used to establish a pecking order and to promote mobility within the organizational social order (Gabriel, 1998). The use of abusive tactics has also been reported among prison inmates as a means of achieving status (Ireland, 2000).

The reward system may encourage supervisors to try to get rid of very high or low performing subordinates (Kräkel, 1997). This might occur if a supervisor perceives a very talented subordinate as a rival and a threat to his own career. In this situation, he might attempt to expel or sabotage the subordinate's work. Supervisor-subordinate bullying may also occur in the opposite case (Kräkel, 1997). When a superior knows that his own rating is based on the performance of his subordinates, a low performing subordinate might be perceived as a liability for the department. The superior may then hope that persistent abuse or harassment will lead the subordinate to either request a transfer or leave the organization. As a result, a reasonable argument can be made that some performance-related pay systems can virtually institutionalize the practice of bad behavior.

It is also possible to see how the adoption of abusive tactics may simply be an efficient way to get things done—a productive part of organizational life that helps to progress the strategic mission (Treadway et al., 2013). Zapf and Warth (1997) have referred to these types of actions as "personnel work by other means". What they mean by this is that abusive tactics are sometimes used to drive unwanted employees out of the corporation who might otherwise be difficult to legally terminate. Similarly, Lee (2000) also noted that these tactics can be used strategically as a way to terminate employees and avoid making severance payments.

The Organizational Systems Perspective

The examination of abusive misconduct thus far has been at the individual or situational level. A third way to consider it is to think about the ways in which it might be completely functional at the organizational level. If it is, it raises these questions: Could bad behavior result from ordinary people operating in organizational circumstances that selectively elicit bad behavior from their natures? Is there some aspect of the "DNA" of organizations—the guiding principles by which companies exist—which tends to promote uncivil behavior resulting in toxic situations? What role does the organizational system play in creating conditions that help to create the conditions ripe for abuse and misconduct? As a framework, we will rely on the three general concepts of organizations outlined by Scott and Davis (2007): *rational* systems, *natural* systems, and *open* systems will be examined next.

Rational Systems

Organizations as rational systems are fundamentally mechanistic and do not seem to know or care about the human consequences of their actions. Highly functional organizations work like well-oiled machines. They are built around roles which can be filled by any properly trained individual. Maximum efficiency leads to maximum productivity, aimed at the goal of maximum profitability. Labor is part of the cost of production, and therefore a factor to be minimized. Human issues not directly related to productivity (e.g. sickness, fatigue, personal concerns, family issues) are additional costs which drain resources. Individuals who cannot fill their roles most efficiently are replaced, just like worn parts.

In the corporate realm, efficiency trumps humanity, and maximizing returns tends to come before family or personal loyalty. Greider (2003, p. 238) suggested that employees are just severable commodities—just another "market input—while the "efficient" corporation keeps its distance from long-term commitments or two-way relationships. He further noted:

> What seems priceless in one realm may be wasted freely or even destroyed by the other. Human experience is sacred to society, a marketable commodity in capitalism ... A conscientious manager shrugs and does his job, carries out the decision, and finds rationales so he can live with himself. If the company doesn't do well, then everybody loses. (p. 35)

Use of abusive tactics in a rational system is not a *necessary* behavior, but it is entirely *rational*. It would be one of many possible ways of "fixing a part" deemed not to be working as desired. A concern about "hurting someone's feelings" is extraneous, at best, in relation to getting assigned work accomplished. While the same results could be achieved in caring and sensitive ways, the point is that purely rational organizations would not focus on the process, but only on the results. As stated by Zimbardo (2008):

> Both public and private organizations, because they operate within a legal framework, not an ethical framework, can inflict suffering, even death, on people by following the cold rationality for achieving the goals of their ideology, a master plan, a cost-benefit equation, or the bottom line of profit. Under those circumstances, their ends always justify efficient means (pp. 381–382).

Only when constrained by laws or regulations, or other external factors which might affect productivity or profitability, would such "soft" factors matter. While the world of business leadership may be populated by decent people, the system currently in place seems to force them to make indecent decisions (Balfour & Fuller, 2010).

Natural Systems

Organizations as natural systems are made up of humans. These humans fill roles, but the roles do not entirely define them. Most importantly, these humans have desires and goals of their own that transcend those of the organization. Humans have needs (e.g. Maslow, 1943), they are motivated by different rewards and punishments, they learn and adapt so that their responses to events change, and they develop over time so that their needs, motivations, and learning continue to evolve.

All of these issues are obvious to most managers in organizations. The difficulty with this framework, though, is that it developed primarily in response to rational systems rather than as the way of understanding organizations and our human relationships to them. It became an overlay of all of those messy, human issues with which organizations have to deal in order to achieve the productivity for which they were designed, but it did not change the fundamental purpose of organizations, or the ways in which they are evaluated. As such, Scott and Davis (2007) suggest the following kinds of criticisms:

> Several decades of research have demonstrated no clear relation between worker satisfaction and productivity…no clear relation between supervisory behavior or leadership style and worker productivity…no clear relation between job enlargement and worker satisfaction or productivity…and no clear relation between participation in decision making and satisfaction or productivity. (p. 69)

An environment focused on human characteristics might seem to be one of the least likely to encourage abusive tactics. That may differ greatly, though, depending on assumptions about human nature and what is "natural". Hierarchies and "pecking orders" appear to be prevalent in most animal groupings, from birds to primates. The concept of the alpha male and competition for positions of dominance are considered normal and necessary to establish order. Those kinds of behaviors in children and adolescents are often considered to be parts of natural development, extending into sports and later into the workplace.

Francis De Waal (2009), a primatologist, strongly challenges the well-established notion of the "law of the jungle". He argues that cooperation is much more prevalent and important in nature—that it accounts much more for survival, in a larger sense, than does competition. As applied to humans and economics, he further explains that the phrase, "survival of the fittest", was actually coined by the British philosopher Herbert Spencer. In fact:

> He said of the poor that "the whole effort of nature is to get rid of such, to clear the world of them, and make room for better" … The United States listened attentively… John D. Rockefeller even married it with religion, concluding that the growth of a large business "is merely the working out of a law of nature and a law of God". (p. 28)

Effectively, then, many such concepts often associated with *natural order* were in fact creations of thinkers focused on humans and organizations but attributed in reverse. Abusive treatment of others might well be considered a natural part of natural systems, but only by using ideas which had been misapplied long ago. And critically, the criteria by which human-focused organizational structures are evaluated are no different than they are for rational systems—simple efficiency and productivity.

Open Systems

Foundational theories for open systems can be found primarily in the work of Ludwig von Bertalanffy (1968) and Andras Angyal (1941). In their simplest form, systems are always and inherently parts of their environments. Systems and their environments co-exist and co-evolve.

Humans have long survived as parts of nature. People organized themselves into companies and corporations for many of the same reasons that early humans organized themselves into hunting parties—it is easier to accomplish more when working together.

Cooperation can be highly useful. Humans learned to harness animals and created tools to do what they could not do with their own hands and backs. There must have been a mental shift, though, when humans began to use other humans as a means of labor like they did animals—that is, as slaves or employees for hire. Rather than cooperating and sharing, people were led and directed.

Having a division of labor, like other forms of cooperation, can be highly functional; however, it requires direction and coordination so that all of these different efforts work together toward a common end. To do this does not necessarily require the bureaucracies and hierarchies which developed (and which still exist). It also does not require oppression or mistreatment of workers in any form.

Farmers coming together for a barn-raising are not inherently less productive than workers in a sweatshop. The Internet, on which much of the world now relies in different ways, still operates through the cooperation of volunteers working for the Internet Engineering Task Force (IETF, Online). This is not to argue for disbanding all current forms of work organizations. It is to say that there is no reason that they have to function exactly as they do, in their current forms, in order to achieve the needed outcomes of cooperative human activity.

The Combined Individual, Situational, and Organizational Systems Perspective

Putting all of this together, it is easy to see how organizations functioning as purely rational systems might cause a leader to treat his or her employees badly, even if simply through ignorance or neglect. Focusing strictly on efficiency, productivity, and profitability does not require civility, empathy, or kindness.

An example might be useful. If a young employee is promoted into a supervisory position, she may (or may not) get the training and mentoring that she needs in order to handle her increased authority. If she becomes aggressive or abusive but is still successful in meeting her goals, her subordinates are likely to suffer. Sadly, though, the situation will probably not be addressed unless management also pays attention to *the way* in which her results were obtained.

Similarly, if a good manager finds himself under pressure and begins treating employees badly, it is purely up to the organization to intervene (or not) given that there are no laws requiring that employees be treated with civility in a private workplace. If we were to require nothing more than this of our workplaces, though, it would be like turning parts of our societies over to functional socio-paths—individuals who simply lack the capacity for empathy with other humans.

In some ways, we have arrived very close to this dilemma. The functional requirements for our workplaces demand no necessary empathy or civility—only productivity. Historically, we have counted on good people of moral character to run our organizations as parts of the larger civil society in which we live and work. When that did not happen, we began "taming" them through laws and regulations. In particular, a large body of statutory, administrative, and common law protections granting various employment rights to individuals emerged during the 1960s and 1970s.

Bright and ambitious people, though, always find ways around regulations (e.g. Weaver & Mathews, 2013). Some learn early that it is much easier to *play the rules* than to *play by the rules*. That is not to say that every employee or manager accused of using abusive tactics is pathological. Given the work environments which we have fostered, there may simply be a combination of too much pressure and too little guidance or boundaries, creating unintended consequences. Human behavior is always subject to situational forces (Zimbardo, 2008; Lewin et al., 1939).

A familiar example of the impact of situational influence is the Stanford Prison Experiment (SPE). In 1971, Philip Zimbardo, a professor at Stanford University at the time, had college students act out the roles of prisoners and guards for a social psychology experiment. The planned two-week study had to be stopped after just six days. The students acting as guards had become sadistic, and student prisoners had become extremely stressed and even depressed.

The SPE results were subsequently replicated—unintentionally—through the behavior of guards and prisoners at the Abu Ghraib prison in Iraq (Hersh,

2004). Zimbardo (2008) was called in as a consultant to help explain what had happened. As he describes what he learned:

> The primary simple lesson that the Stanford Prison Experiment teaches is that *situations matter* [emphasis added]. Social situations can have more profound effects on the behavior and mental functioning of individuals, groups, and national leaders than we might believe possible. Some situations can exert such powerful influence over us that we can be led to behave in ways we would not, could not, predict was possible in advance (pp. 211–212).

Zimbardo further explains the power of roles which can often be set aside as individuals move between settings. If the roles are strongly internalized, though, they can change the nature of a person's identity. In so doing, they can shape new behavior, including the violation of previously held morals and values. The more strongly the new behaviors are rewarded, the more likely they are to continue. As Zimbardo (2008) summarizes his findings:

> The most important lesson to be derived from the SPE is that Situations are created by Systems. Systems provide the institutional support, authority, and resources that allow Situations to operate as they do…System Power involves authoritarian or institutionalized permission to behave in prescribed ways or to forbid or punish actions that are contrary to them. It provides the "higher authority" that gives validation to playing new roles, following new rules, and taking "actions that would ordinarily be constrained by pre-existing laws, norms, morals, and ethics." Such validation usually comes cloaked in the mantle of ideology. (p. 226)

It is true that organizational systems have enormous power to resist change. That said, it is equally true that through awareness, guidance, and new policies and laws, it is possible for at least some people to learn new approaches. Regardless of the reasons for disrespectful or uncivil interactions at work, in the end, treating employees abusively is simply not acceptable in a civil society. For now, the magnitude and ubiquity of this type of poor treatment remains a key reason that employees so often experience toxic emotions at work—and why practitioners like you are so often left to pick up the pieces.

References

Anderson, C., Brion, S., Moore, D., & Kennedy, J. (2012, October). A status-enhancement account of overconfidence. *Journal of Personality and Social Psychology, 103*(4), 718–735.

Andersson, L. M., & Pearson, C. M. (1999). Tit for tat? The spiraling effect of incivility in the workplace. *Academy of Management Review, 24*, 452–471.

Angyal, A. (1941). *Foundations for a science of personality.* New York: The Commonwealth Fund.

Babiak, P., & Hare, R. D. (2006). *Snakes in suits.* New York: Harper Collins.

Balfour, A., & Fuller, S. (2010). Why business leaders are profit motivated rather than socially motivated: The role of business education. *The Journal of Global Business Management, 6*(2), 191–197.

Bandura, A. (1973). *Aggression: A social learning analysis.* Englewood Cliffs, NJ: Prentice Hall.

Bertalanffy, L. (1968). *General system theory* (Rev. ed.) New York: George Braziller.

Boddy, C. R. (2011). *Corporate psychopaths: Organisational destroyers.* New York: Palgrave Macmillan.

Brodsky, C. (1976). *The harassed worker.* Lexington, MA: Lexington Books.

Center for Advanced Human Resource Studies. (2012, February). *Do nice guys—and gals—really finish last? The joint effects of sex and agreeableness on income* (CAHRS Research Link No. 18). Ithaca, NY: Cornell University, ILR School.

Cheng, J. T., Tracy, J. L., Foulsham, T., Kingstone, A., & Henrich, J. (2013). Two ways to the top: Evidence that dominance and prestige are distinct yet viable avenues to social rank and influence. *Journal of Personality & Social Psychology, 104*(1), 103–125.

Collinson, D. (1988). *Managing the shop floor: Subjectivity, masculinity and workplace culture.* Berlin: Walter de Gruyter & Co.

Crawshaw, L. (2005). *Coaching abrasive executives: Exploring the use of empathy in constructing less destructive interpersonal management strategies.* Doctoral dissertation, Fielding Graduate University. Retrieved from http://www.bosswhispering.com/Coaching-Abrasive-Executives.pdf.

Crawshaw, L. (2007). *Taming the abrasive manager.* San Francisco, CA: Jossey-Bass.

Daniel, T. A. (2009). *"Tough boss" or workplace bully: A grounded theory study of insights from human resource professionals.* Doctoral dissertation, Fielding Graduate University. Retrieved from http://gradworks.umi.com/33/50/3350585.html.

De Waal, F. (2009). *The age of empathy: Nature's lessons for a kinder society.* New York: Harmony.

DiSalvo, D. (2012). *Why jerks get ahead.* Retrieved from http://www.forbes.com/sites/daviddisalvo/2012/08/18/why-jerks-get-ahead/.

Einarsen, S., & Raknes, B. (1997). Harassment in the workplace and the victimization of men. *Violence and Victims, 12*(3), 247–263.

Einarsen, S., Raknes, B., & Matthiesen, S. (1994). Bullying and harassment at work and their relationships to work environment quality: An exploratory study. *European Work & Organizational Psychologist, 4*(4), 381–401.

Einarsen, S., Schanke, M., Aasland, M., & Skogstad, A. (2007). Destructive leadership: A definition and conceptual model. *Leadership Quarterly, 3*, 207–216.

Ford, C. (2005). *Against the grain: An irreverent view of Alberta*. Toronto: McLelland & Stewart Ltd.

Furnham, A. (2009). Narcissism at work: The narcissistic personality and organizational relationships. In R. Morrison & S. Wright (Eds.), *Friends and enemies in organizations: A work psychology perspective* (pp. 168–194). New York, NY: Palgrave Macmillan.

Gabriel, Y. (1998). An introduction to the social psychology of insults in organizations. *Human Relations, 5*(11), 1329–1354.

Greider, W. (2003). *The soul of capitalism: Opening paths to a moral economy*. New York: Simon & Schuster.

Hare, R. D. (1993). *Without conscience: The disturbing world of psychopaths among us*. New York: The Guilford Press.

Hearn, J., & Parkin, W. (2001). *Gender, sexuality and violence in organizations*. London: Sage.

Hersh, S. M. (2004, May 10). Torture at Abu Ghraib. *The New Yorker*. Retrieved from http://www.newyorker.com/archive/2004/05/10/040510fa_fact.

Hoel, H., & Cooper, C. (2000). *Destructive conflict and bullying at work*. Manchester, UK: University of Manchester Institute of Science and Technology.

Hoel, H., & Salin, D. (2003). Organizational antecedents of workplace bullying. In S. Einarsen, H. Hoel, D. Zapf, & C. Cooper (Eds.), *Bullying and emotional abuse in the workplace: International perspectives in research and practice*. London: Taylor & Francis.

Horn, S. (2002). *Take the bully by the horns: Stop unethical, uncooperative, or unpleasant people from running and ruining your life*. New York: St. Martin's Griffin.

Hornstein, H. A. (1996). *Brutal bosses and their prey: How to identify and overcome abuse in the workplace*. New York: Riverhead Books.

Internet Engineering Task Force. Retrieved from http://www.ietf.org/.

Ireland, J. L. (2000). 'Bullying' among prisoners: A review of research. *Aggression and Violent Behavior, 5*(2), 201–215.

Johns, N., & Menzel, P. J. (1999). 'If you can't stand the heat!'… kitchen violence and culinary art. *Hospitality Management, 18*, 99–109.

Kaplan, R. (1991). *Beyond ambition*. San Francisco, CA: Jossey-Bass.

Kräkel, M. (1997). Rent-seeking in organisationen- eine okonomishe analyse sozial schadlichen verhaltens. *Schmalenbachs Zeitschrift fur Betriebswirtschaftliche Forschung, 49*(6), 535–555.

Kramer, R. M. (2006). The great intimidators. *Harvard Business Review*. Retrieved from http://hbr.org/2006/02/the-great-intimidators/ar/1.

Lee, D. (2000). An analysis of workplace bullying in the UK. *Personnel Review, 29*(5), 593–610.
Levinson, H. (1978, May–June). The abrasive personality. *Harvard Business Review*, 86–94.
Lewin, K., Lippitt, R., & White, R. (1939). Patterns of aggressive behaviour in experimentally created social climates. *Journal of Social Psychology, 10*, 271–299.
Leymann, H. (1990). Mobbing and psychological terror at workplaces. *Violence and Victims, 52*, 119–126.
Leymann, H. (1996). The content and development of mobbing at work. *European Journal of Work and Organizational Psychology, 5*(2), 165–184.
Livingston, R. W. S. (2001). *Bias in the absence of malice: The phenomenon of unintentional discrimination*. Unpublished doctoral dissertation, The Ohio State University.
Lubit, R. (2004). *Coping with toxic managers, subordinates ... and other difficult people.* Upper Saddle River, NJ: Financial Times Press.
Ludeman, K., & Erlandson, E. (2006). *Alpha male syndrome*. Boston, MA: Harvard Business School Press.
Maslow, A. H. (1943). A theory of human motivation. *Psychological Review, 50*(4), 370–396. Retrieved from http://psychclassica.yorku.ca/Maslow/motivation.htm
Neuman, J., & Baron, R. (2011). Social antecedents of bullying: A social interactionist perspective. In S. Einarsen, H. Hoel, D. Zapf, & C. Cooper (Eds.), *Bullying and harassment in the workplace: Developments in theory, research, and practice* (pp. 149–174). New York, NY: CRC Press.
Nunberg, G. (2012a, August 15). *Why do we idolize jerks?* Retrieved from http://www.alternet.org/culture/why-do-we-idolize-jerks.
Nunberg, G. (2012b). *Ascent of the A-word: Assholism, the first sixty years*. New York: Public Affairs/Perseus Books.
O'Leary-Kelly, A. M., Griffin, R. W., & Glew, D. J. (1996). Organization-motivated aggression: A research framework. *Academy of Management Review, 21*(1), 225–253.
O'Moore, M. (2000). *Summary report on the national survey on workplace bullying in Ireland*. Dublin: The Anti-Bullying Research Centre, Trinity College.
Pearson, C., & Porath, C. (2009). *The cost of bad behavior*. New York, NY: Penguin Books.
Peck, M. S. (1998). *People of the lie: The hope for healing human evil*. New York: Touchtone.
Rogers, K. (2011, November 3). *Why being the office jerk could pay off*. Retrieved from http://www.foxbusiness.com/personal-finance/2011/11/03/workplace-jerks-make-more-money/#ixzz2NMghSBqR.
Salin, D. (2003). Ways of explaining workplace bullying: A review of enabling, motivating, and precipitating structures and processes in the work environment. *Human Relations, 56*(10), 1213–1232.
Schouten, R., & Silver, J. (2012). *Almost a psychopath: Do I (or does someone I know) have a problem with manipulation and lack of empathy?* Center City, MN: Hazelden.

Scott, W. R., & Davis, G. F. (2007). *Organizations and organizing: Rational, natural and open system perspectives*. Upper Saddle River, NJ: Pearson.

Sewell, G., & Wilkinson, B. (1992). Empowerment or emasculation? Shop floor surveillance in a total quality organization. In P. Blyton & P. Turnbull (Eds.), *Reassessing human resource management*. London: SAGE.

Sperry, L. (2009). Mobbing and bullying: A consulting psychology perspective and overview. *Consulting Psychology Journal, 61*(3), 190–201.

Thylefors, I. (1987). *Scapegoats: On expulsion and bullying in working life*. Stockholm: Natur och Kultur.

Treadway, D. C., Shaughnessy, B. A., Breland, J. W., Yang, J., & Reeves, M. (2013). Political skill and the job performance of bullies. *Journal of Managerial Psychology, 28*(3), 273–289.

Van Kleef, M., Homan, G. A., Finkenauer, A. C., Gundemir, S., & Stamkon, E. (2011). Breaking the rules to rise to power: How norm violators gain power in the eyes of others. *Social Psychological and Personality Science, 2*(5), 500–507.

Weaver, C., & Mathews, A. W. (2013, May 20). Employers eye bare-bones health plans under new law. *The Wall Street Journal*. Retrieved from http://online.wsj.com/article/SB10001424127887324787004578493274030598186.html.

Zapf, D., & Einarsen, S. (2011). Individual antecedents of bullying: Victims and perpetrators. In S. Einarsen, H. Hoel, D. Zapf, & C. Cooper (Eds.), *Bullying and harassment in the workplace: Developments in theory, research and practice* (pp. 177–200). New York, NY: CRC Press.

Zapf, D., & Warth, K. (1997). Bullying: Warfare in the workplace. *Psychologie Heute, 24*(8), 20–24, 28–29.

Zimbardo, P. (2008). *The Lucifer effect: Understanding how good people turn evil*. New York: Random House Trade Paperbacks.

4

What Causes Toxic Workplace Situations? A Focus on the Ethical Drivers

Another common driver of organizational toxicity is created by the ethical lapses of senior leaders. As they rise within their organizations, there are fewer "guard rails" in the form of checks and balances on their decision-making and actions. When their policy infractions or personal infidelities come to light, there are consequences that not only affect the leader and his or her family, but that also impact employees who may suffer long after the individual has been replaced.

It is a fair question to ask why highly intelligent people are so often seduced into taking more risks and making poor decisions just when they have achieved great organizational success and have the most to lose—what has been referred to as the *paradox of success* when applied to business leaders (Daniel, 2013). Let me explain by providing some context for the types of influences that they are likely to encounter, and some rationale about why they so often succumb to these temptations.

We live in a society that makes celebrities of successful people in sports, politics, business, and government only to find that they are not really what they have advertised themselves to be. With only a cursory scan of recent news reports, it is very easy to identify many more high-profile people who have been involved in very public scandals in recent years. Prominent individuals like Lance Armstrong, Tiger Woods, John Edwards, and former President Bill Clinton immediately come to mind. You can undoubtedly recall numerous other recent scandals as well. While it is relatively easy to find short-term heroes, it is becoming increasingly difficult to find leaders who can sustain our respect over the course of a long and distinguished career. This is especially true in a world that can publicly broadcast indiscretions and errors of judgment with almost lightning speed. All it takes is a Tweet or a text.

Accounting fraud, embezzlement, tax evasion, bid rigging, over-billing, substance abuse, sexual impropriety, and perjury top the list of indiscretions most frequently leading to the downfall of successful executives. Leaders who were at one time the focus of admiration by the press regularly appear on the cover of business magazines reporting on their removal from senior positions with headlines like *Flameout* or *What Went Wrong?* Others face messy public trials, government investigations, corporate audits, or costly divorces as a result of their actions. The public is no longer surprised by reports of these reckless acts; sadly, we have almost come to expect them. It has become harder and harder to find honest and ethical men and women to emulate—those with high integrity who really are in private who they publicly claim to be.

Unexpected and high-level departures due to ethical violations are transitions which tend to create organizational toxicity. These events are usually unexpected and cause tumultuous times for both management and employees alike. Everyone has to work through the rumors and gossip-mongering to figure out the "new normal" once the executive has departed and the fire has died down. Once new leaders are selected, personalities often collide. With a "new sheriff in town" doing it his or her new way, it is not surprising that conflict can arise and escalate, causing a new set of toxic emotions to be created within the affected group. If the issues are not resolved quickly, the problem mounts and employees may decide to leave or, worse yet, become unproductive but stay in place.

So, What Makes Leaders Fail?

There are numerous personal and organizational benefits that typically go along with success: increasing levels of power, influence, rewards, status, and control of resources. However, history confirms that high-level achievement can often come with a fairly hefty price tag (Kelly, 1988). Some of the more common reasons for ethical failures include.

Privileged Access

When a person becomes highly successful at work, he or she typically gains greater power and influence, increased status (both internally and externally), a heightened sense of personal achievement, plus greater perks and financial rewards. These personal benefits of success are collectively referred to as *privileged access* (Ludwig & Longenecker, 1993). In addition to these personal gains, the successful leader generally is given greater control of resources and decision processes, increased access to information, people, and resources, and the ability to set their own agendas without direct day-to-day supervision.

Lack of Balance

As corporate executives climb the corporate ladder, an inability to share their problems, hopes, and dreams, coupled with large blocks of time away from home, can cause them to experience a sense of increasing personal isolation and a lack of intimacy in their relationships (Berglas, 1986). It can also lead them to become somewhat out of touch with reality (Kets de Vries, 1989; Berglas, 1986).

I Want It All—And I Want It Now

As leaders become more successful, they frequently become more "emotionally expansive" with an almost insatiable appetite for increased markers of success, thrills, gratification, and control (Blotnick, 1987). Jim Collins (2009) refers to it as "the undisciplined pursuit of more". Once this level of success has been achieved, executives often lose their ability to be satisfied with their current status and desire more and more of the trappings of success (e.g. a McMansion in the most exclusive gated neighborhood, expensive cars and jewelry, private schools for their children, customized boats, second or third homes).

Stress and a Heightened Fear of Failure

Once successful, leaders often become increasingly stressed and fearful about not achieving their goals, leading to constant anxiety and concern about the future (Ludwig & Longenecker, 1993) Coupled with the increasing isolation commonly experienced as a by-product of organizational success, executives can find themselves in a very lonely and discontented situation. All too often, their loneliness and sense of isolation are not off-set by the tangible rewards and status associated with their position.

Inflated Ego and a Sense of Exemption from Rules

All of the trappings that come with corporate success can collude to make a leader develop an "inflated sense of personal ability to manipulate outcomes" (Ludwig & Longenecker, 1993). This egocentricity can cause the leader to become abrasive, close-minded, disrespectful, and prone to extreme displays of negative emotion. This sense of personal infallibility has been referred to as the "I am the center of the universe phenomenon" (Blotnick, 1987).

A similar phenomenon has been confirmed by Price (2000, 2006) who suggested that "leadership induces and maintains a leader's belief that he is somehow exempt from the moral requirements that apply to the rest of us". This can cause a leader to subconsciously develop a belief that while there is a mandatory set of rules for most people, there is a different (and less restrictive) set of rules governing the executive.

The "Emptiness Syndrome"

After working for years and finally achieving senior levels of responsibility and all that comes with it, leaders often take a step back and ask themselves "is this all there is to success?" (Berglas, 1986). When they have exceeded their own career expectations in terms of position, pay, and perks, there is little else left for them to strive for on a professional level. Research suggests that these are typically hard-charging executives who have been engaged in a relentless pursuit of goals and results during their entire career. If there is nothing left to strive for, they often stop and ask themselves *what's the point?* The lack of new goals can undermine the early enthusiasm and clarity of purpose that led to their success in the first place. It is at that point that boredom can set in which can stimulate the executive to take more risks or become distracted from doing the work of the organization.

Early Strengths Become Later Weaknesses

Conger (1990) suggested that most people experience a duality in their lives. Steve Jobs, the now-deceased former CEO and founder of Apple Computer, is a recent example of a very public business leader with a prominent duality attached to his legacy. In fact, the August cover of *Wired* magazine (Austen, 2012) shows a photograph of Jobs sporting both a halo and horns along with a provocative story title that read: "Do you *really* want to be like Steve Jobs?"

According to those who knew him best, he was a brilliant innovator and good friend; to others, he was a tyrant and a jerk. Apparently, both perspectives were absolutely on target depending on the situation and the person. As a result, his life story serves as an inspiration for some and a cautionary tale for others (Austen, 2012). It is the very strengths that a leader is treasured and admired for that can become a liability under the right circumstances, especially during times of stress (Maccoby, 2003). These potential but latent weaknesses have often been referred to as "the dark side of leadership" (Conger, 1990; McIntosh & Rima, 1997).

It is often at the top that an executive will self-destruct by taking action that they know is perilous, yet they arrogantly believe that they have the power to conceal it and not get caught. So, despite the acknowledged risk, they engage in the dangerously risky action anyway. Why? Either the leader becomes bored and arrogantly expects that the misdeeds will not be discovered or he or she becomes convinced that it is deserved repayment for prior sacrifices (LaBier, 1986).

Ironically, it is the most successful leaders that tend to suffer the worst ethical dilemmas (Ciulla, 1998, 2004). Equally ironic is the fact that most leaders dethroned by scandal have had a long and distinguished history of honest and loyal service to their organization. This is why their precipitous falls from grace are generally so shocking and unexpected to those who know them well.

Corporate Culture Drives Bad Behaviors

Some industries seem to be based on a culture of greed and excess: as an example, think Wall Street. The finance industry represents capitalism in its purest form—the single-minded pursuit of profit. As the 2008 financial crisis confirmed, it appears that our financial structure in the United States is predicated on a system which colludes to drive bad behavior (Boddy, 1976). It is a system based on poor risk controls, massive leverage, egregious financial rewards, predatory lending practices, the purchase of influence, and a complete lack of any sense of fiduciary responsibility to the ultimate client (Greycourt, 2008).

Many commentators have suggested that the root cause of the 2008 crisis was the gradual collapse of ethical behavior across the financial industry. Financial firms began to behave in ways that were in their (and especially their top executives) short-term interest without any concern about the longer-term impact on the industry's customers, on the broader American economy, or even on the firm's own employees.

In just the past decade alone, Wells Fargo Bank settled a toxic mortgage investments case for $6.5 million (Protess, 2012), while Standard Chartered has agreed to settle allegations by New York state regulators that they engaged in money laundering for $340 million (Tangel, 2012). JP Morgan projected staggering losses in excess of $9 billion due to risky trading strategies which included an oversized bet on credit derivatives (Silver-Greenburg & Craig, 2012). Within such a context, it is relatively easy to understand the significant temptation that exists for executives to make decisions that have the potential to increase their personal bonuses and rewards, but which are not necessarily in the best interest of their company or client.

Conclusions

It would be a mistake to assume that it is only individuals who are morally corrupt or unprincipled who fall victim to ethical violations. To the contrary, the paradox of success is that it is the smartest people in the room—those who are the *most* talented and successful—that tend to inexplicably self-destruct at the very peak of their career.

The intersection of success and the potential for risky actions by leaders is clearly a dangerous crossroad. Extreme personal autonomy at work—coupled with the likely egotism and arrogance that comes from a history of success—sets up a potentially disastrous dynamic. Despite an illustrious career—so far—it is important for leaders (and this includes HR practitioners too) to understand that they can quickly lose it all if they give in to the inevitable temptations waiting for them at the top.

Organizational "guard rails" are needed to help executives avoid these temptations in the form of policies, procedures, and increased oversight (Daniel, 2021; Nielsen, 1987). If left to their own devices and allowed to make decisions without appropriate checks and balances, senior leaders will often make poor choices that will ultimately result in their termination and generate bad publicity for their organization. A hyper-focused awareness of these enticements, both by HR and senior leaders, will go a long way toward decreasing the toxic spillover to employees and the organization that is an inevitable consequence of these types of common (and entirely too frequent) ethical lapses.

References

Austen, B. (2012, August). Do you *really* want to be like Steve Jobs? *Wired Magazine*. Retrieved from https://www.cultofmac.com/180287/wireds-new-cover-asks-if-you-really-want-to-be-like-steve-jobs/.

Berglas, S. (1986). *The success syndrome: Hitting bottom when you reach the top*. New York: Plenum Press.

Blotnick, S. (1987). *Ambitious men: Their drives, dreams, and delusions*. New York: Viking.

Boddy, C. (1976). *Corporate psychopaths: Organisational destroyers*. New York: Palgrave Macmillan.

Ciulla, J. B. (1998). *Ethics: The heart of leadership*. Westport, CT: Praeger.

Ciulla, J. B. (2004). Ethics and leadership effectiveness. In J. Antonakis, A. T. Cianciolo, & R. J. Sternberg (Eds.), *The nature of leadership* (pp. 302–327). Thousand Oaks: Sage Publications.

Collins, J. (2009). *How the mighty fall*. Collins Business Essentials.

Conger, J. (1990). The dark side of leadership. *Organizational Dynamics, 19*, 44–55.

Daniel, T. A. (2013, Summer). *Executive success and the increased potential for ethical failure*. SHRM Legal Report. SHRM, Alexandria, VA. Retrieved from http://www.shrm.org/publications/pages/default.aspx.

Daniel, T. A. (2021). *Guardrails: Taming toxic leaders and building positive cultures*. Alexandria, VA: SHRM Books.

Greycourt. (2008). *The financial crisis and the collapse of ethical behavior*. Greycourt Whitepaper No. 44. Pittsburgh, PA: Greycourt & Co.

Kelly, C. M. (1988). *The destructive achiever*. Reading, MA: Addison-Wesley.

Kets de Vries, M. F. (1989). Leaders who self-destruct: The causes and cures. *Organizational Dynamics, 17*, 5–17.

LaBier, D. (1986). *Modern madness: The emotional fallout of success*. Reading, MA: Addison-Wesley.

Ludwig, D. C., & Longenecker, C. O. (1993). The "Bathsheba syndrome": The ethical failure of successful leaders. *Journal of Business Ethics, 12*, 265–273.

Maccoby, M. (2003). *The productive narcissist: The promise and peril of visionary leadership*. New York: Broadway Books.

McIntosh, G. L., & Rima, S. D. (1997). *Overcoming the dark side of leadership: The paradox of personal dysfunction*. Grand Rapids, MI: Baker Books.

Nielsen, R. P. (1987). What can managers do about unethical management? *Journal of Business Ethics, 4*, 65–70.

Price, T. L. (2000). Explaining ethical failures of leadership. *The Leadership & Organization Development Journal, 12*, 177–184.

Price, T. L. (2006). *Understanding ethical failures in leadership*. Cambridge, MA: Cambridge University Press.

Protess, B. (2012, August 14). Wells Fargo settles mortgage investments case for $6.5 million. *New York Times*. Retrieved from http://dealbook.nytimes.com/2012/08/14/wells-fargo-settles-mortgage-investments-case-for-6-5-million/

Silver-Greenburg, J., & Craig, S. (2012, August 14). JP Morgan trading loss may exceed $9 billion. *The New York Times*. Retrieved from http://dealbook.nytimes.com/2012/06/28/jpmorgan-trading-loss-may-reach-9-billion/

Tangel, A. (2012, August 14). Standard Chartered to pay $340 million in money-laundering case. *Los Angeles Times*. Retrieved from http://www.latimes.com/business/money/la-fi-mo-standard-chartered-settles-new-york-case-20120814,0,6816539.story

5

Why They Do It

There are two prevalent, but divergent, views about why HR practitioners tend to take on organizational toxin handling responsibilities. Some are of the opinion that HR professionals are typically caring individuals who are both empathetic listeners and problem solvers by nature. This combination of traits both draws them to the HR profession and causes employees to seek their counsel—suggesting that innate personality characteristics compel practitioners to take on these duties. Others opine that dealing with employee struggles is simply an inherent part of the role of HR itself. Each of these positions will be examined next.

Innate Personality Characteristics

Some practitioners are of the opinion that it is a personal choice to take on the toxin handling role due to the personality characteristics of most HR practitioners. They suggest that most individuals who choose HR as a profession do so as a result of their empathetic and compassionate natures and because of their ability to solve problems (Daniel, 2018). In their own words:

> *I think some people are inherently more empathetic than others. I've found over the last 20 years working at HR that a lot of those people tend to gravitate towards the HR role [because] they want to take care of everybody. They want to take care of people and, because of that, they become the toxin handler.*

So, I really believe some in HR choose [it] because they have a passion and a certain degree of empathy with regard to working with human capital. They have an understanding of the rights and roles of both management and employees and how each of those must be treated with respect and dignity to ensure mutually beneficial relationships, healthy environments, and successful outcomes.

I think it's a natural tendency for people who like this type of work [to be] empathetic people, but I also think they could take their empathy elsewhere. There are lots of other jobs in the world where empathy is a very important piece but if a person is in business, I think perhaps they would lean more towards this field [HR].

I think some people just by nature want to help or nurture people, want to listen and offer advice and guidance.

HR practitioners often have a "calling to listen and to help". They have a personality of caring that causes them to get drawn to the role.

HR practitioners are generally empathetic people who are good listeners. HR wants to help—they even make "house calls" and try to be available to employees at all hours.

My opinion is that some people have the natural ability and some people don't. And you can have you know two people in the same position in HR and one of them can do it and one of them can't—it's just empathy. I do think that, in general, people who are empathetic are more likely to be in an HR type of position because they do like to help people ... so they gravitate towards it [the role] kind of naturally.

Everyone sees HR as "the emotions people". So I think very often managers in some other functional areas don't feel like they have the aptitude to deal with those kinds of things and they call on us because they see it as more of an HR role—that we're more of the "touchy feely" person. I always used to joke it made me nuts people always were like oh "HR's just paychecks and parties"—like we don't do serious stuff, I do think that people always see anything that's touchy feely as an HR thing. You've got to pull them in. I'm not doing this by myself.

Requirement of the Role

Others suggest that toxin handling is simply an inherent part of the HR role itself (regardless whether or not it is included in their official job description). In smaller organizations, HR tends to be "everything to everyone"; in larger organizations, the roles tend to be more defined and explicit.

> There is a built-in assumption that HR is the "people person" who everyone can come to, so naturally the brunt of the emotional issues faced by employees hit HR professionals. They are designated to help employees with issues. And there is an assumption that HR can fix it … [because] they are trained to handle conflict and stress. Employees know/understand this which is why they seek HR's counsel.
>
> It's just part of the job and HR practitioners "step up to the plate" to do what must be done.
>
> So not only are they coming to you based on your role, but they come to you based on advice given or your ability to provide advice.
>
> I think they have an invested relationship with these employees or leaders … so that they are willing to act and address that pain and suffering in employees …so they do it [they take on the pain] because of their commitment, that drive, that relationship built within the organization with those different employees and leaders.
>
> I think the reason why [HR is a toxin handler] is because it's a natural place to go. People are hired by human resources so that's their first point of contact. So naturally if the employee is facing difficulty in their position or if they're facing termination or anything of that nature, HR is where the hiring begins so I think that it is natural that they come to us looking for solutions and looking for a response, assuming that we know what's going on with the organization.
>
> I think our scope is very broad as opposed to other professions …I just feel like we're involved in so many different aspects of an employee's employment experience—we're involved from the moment they are offered a job offer all the way through their retirement (and everything in between). So if they have any discipline issues, if they have any benefit issues, if they have leave issues, or if something changes with their position or with the organization and they're being RIF'd, I just feel like the due to the life cycle of what we work in, I think we have a disproportionate amount of opportunities to be involved in these sorts of things simply due to the nature of our work.

HR Practitioners Are Strongly Identified with Their Work and Tend to Protect Others

These perspectives are consistent with the findings of Davenport, Schwartz, and Elliott (2005) who found that people who experience high levels of organizational toxicity are often individuals who "love their work" and "are identified strongly with what they do". They explained further:

Employees who are committed to their work are often very loyal. They believe in the goals of the organization. They care about the organization's reputation. They keep quiet, are ambivalent about taking action and may not readily seek assistance, inside or outside the organization. They suffer for a longer period. Rarely do such individuals reveal their personal agony. (p. 82)

Practitioners are typically passionate about their role as an HR professional, and will often endure organizational toxicity for an extended period, most often to protect other employees (Daniel, 2012). In their words:

*HR serves as a "serious buffer" for other employees in the organization—between management and employees. We are the **"organizational shock absorbers"**.*

If HR professionals won't stand up to a bad manager, who will? But HR pays a heavy price for doing that.

We put up with a lot because we're in the people business. We take abuse all of the time.

HR practitioners are often willing to stay in a bad situation to protect other employees, only going forward to take action "when it is not just about me anymore".

Understanding this tendency to identify with the work and protect others may help practitioners to more quickly take action to shield themselves from toxic leaders. It may also help them to either resolve or leave unhealthy situations before any long-term damage is done to either their reputation or self-confidence.

Where do you fall on this issue—are the duties of an organizational toxin handler an innate personality characteristic or simply embedded in the organizational role itself? Regardless of your general perspective, the reality is that you are undoubtedly frequently called upon to deal with many problems and decisions made by your organization which, in the aggregate, tend to combust to create organizational toxicity which negatively affects employees and the organization.

Positive Impact of the Role on Toxin Handlers

Although the negative effects of toxin handling on HR practitioners engaged in the work are many, it is possible that being engaged in this type of work can also create some positive benefits. How? The time spent helping others resulted in some practitioners finding a greater sense of meaning and purpose in their work, and results in a higher sense of professionalism, self-efficacy, and overall feelings of positive self-worth.

> *Not to sound obnoxious, but I do it because I know I'm good at it, better than most people. And although it may take its toll [on me personally], I would rather be the one doing it because I know, at the end of the day, I can probably provide that employee with a better bad experience than most other people in the organization [can]. I feel like it's a kindness [to employees] and I also know that, being in HR, you do it more than a line manager ... so you have a level of expertise developed that other managers don't have.*

> *HR's job is to fix things that disrupt the workflow. That takes a lot of energy. It is depleting, but it's always highly rewarding.*

> *I think because we deal with all the crap professionally it deepens a lot of our relationships [with employees and senior leaders] because some of the worst days people may have had, they've had them shoulder to shoulder with me and I've helped them through it.*

Some HR practitioners report feeling engaged and energized by the heavy reliance on their HR services by both senior leaders and employees (Daniel, 2018). This undoubtedly has something to do with their strong desire to fix problems and help people. It is also likely influenced by whether or not they believe that management and employees appreciate their efforts.

> *It really depends on the HR professional you are talking to whether they feel it's a dumping ground or whether they feel like it's engaging them more in the organization.*

So while this section is quite short, it is worth noting that there are, in fact, some inadvertent positive benefits enjoyed by HR practitioners who feel that their organizational presence is valued and appreciated. I hope that maybe you feel it too.

References

Daniel, T. A. (2012, Spring). Caught in the crossfire: When HR practitioners become targets of bullying. *Employment Relations Today, 39*(1), 9–16.

Daniel, T. A. (2018). *Managing toxic emotions at work: An empirical study of HR's role and its Impact on personal well-being and organizational effectiveness.* https://doi.org/10.13140/RG.2.2.16315.26408.

Davenport, N., Schwartz, R., & Elliott, G. (2005). *Mobbing: Emotional abuse in the American workplace.* Ames, IA: Civil Society Publishing.

6

How They Reduce Organizational Pain

Toxin handlers engage in six core activities when they are helping employees and the organization deal with toxic emotions at work. These actions include empathetic listening, suggest solutions and provide resources, work behind the scene and provide a safe space, strategic communication and reframe difficult messages, as well as to advise and coach managers (Daniel, 2018, 2019a, 2019b, 2019c; Frost, 2003, 2004, 2006).

Each of these core activities is discussed separately and supported by excerpts from interviews with experienced HR practitioners interviewed during a recent study (Daniel, 2018).

Empathetic Listening

Toxin handlers take the time to actively listen to an employee's pain and provide an important moment of human connection. Making sure that the person feels "heard" and understood can help to validate their feelings and give employees a greater sense of being valued and respected by the organization.

> *We must be prepared to deal with sadness, anger, and pain resulting from corporate decisions (even some that we may have been involved in helping to make).*
>
> *So, my experience is to … first be a listener. When somebody comes in agitated or emotionally upset, they can't even hear anything you say yet until they finish speaking and getting everything out. So, I always felt it was my role to just be a listener and provide for them a safe environment where they could speak freely and where confidence was maintained.*

Suggest Solutions and Provide Resources

The HR toxin handler looks for ways to resolve, reduce, or manage the emotions being experienced by the employee in pain. This may take the form of brainstorming possible solutions, role-playing difficult conversations, or simply talking about the problem in greater depth. They often have to provide solutions to both management and employees about the same situation, and their dual counsel can cause them to experience internal conflict. In most employee situations, though, employees mostly just need to vent their feelings to someone who will listen.

Not all emotions that HR deals with are caused by work-related decisions, though. Employees also show up to discuss a variety of personal struggles as well—ranging from relationship issues to health problems, and everything in between. Although management does not consider this active listening to be part of the practitioner's primary HR role, it requires a significant portion of their time. How often has an employee stopped by your office, stuck their head in your doorway, and said "Got a minute?" And how many times has that "minute" turned into an hour or more? If your experience is anything like mine, those repeating patterns of interactions with employees confirm that emotions are messy and complex—and take a great deal of time to sort out.

> *People bring conflicts to work from outside of work. HR must explore ways to give them the resources needed to help them with their personal struggles.*
>
> *I don't think people realize that I'm not just dealing with people's work stuff. In the last sixty days I've had two people come in to see me broken about infidelities in their marriage, or problems they're having. I mean people trust me about issues pertaining to custody or all kinds of stuff so it's not always about workplace stuff... I think HR professionals deal with a lot more of that than people appreciate because it's not just the business stuff. People come to us with their personal issues all the time.*

Work Behind the Scenes and Provide a "Safe Space"

The work of the toxin handler most always happens behind the scenes—as a result, it is mostly invisible to senior leaders and others in the organization. The reality is, however, that HR practitioners make it possible (and safe) for employees to vent their frustration or concerns in a confidential setting behind closed doors.

These conversations are often highly personal and emotional. While the work is very important, it is (of necessity) invisible to others making it feel pretty thankless. Despite this lack of value placed on the work, HR professionals still take on this role because they genuinely care about the well-being of their employees *and* the organization.

> So I've found that you have to listen, you have to make it safe, you have to repeat, and then you have to clarify what they're saying ... you have to try and give them a different perspective on the situation or give them encouragement ... whatever the case may be.

They also protect employees in tough situations by helping to facilitate internal transfers or, in particularly intolerable situations, even helping them to find a new job outside of the company.

Confidential Counseling

Employees experiencing intense emotions or who are in a difficult situation frequently find it comforting to talk about their problems in a confidential setting to someone who will listen attentively. As a result, establishing and maintaining a sense of trust is of paramount importance for toxin handlers when working with employees in such situations. Employees must be absolutely certain that HR will keep their confidence.

This need to keep things confidential can place HR in a difficult situation. Why? Because the reality is that HR supports both management *and* also employees. Even if the employee discusses information that may not be the most favorable to management, confidentiality must still be maintained (e.g. an employee who discloses that he or she is leaving the company and wants to discuss their benefits).

> *HR must honor confidentiality but help the employee to problem-solve.*
>
> *I think part of the critical nature of the role is that you maintain confidentiality.*

Strategize Communications and Reframe Difficult Messages

Developing a communication plan and regularly communicating news to employees—both good and bad—is a critical responsibility of most practitioners in the HR role. The overriding goal of the function is to minimize employee stress by keeping the workforce as informed as possible about difficult organizational decisions—with a particular focus on providing answers up-front about who, what, when, where, and, most particularly, *why* the decision was being made.

Reducing the "unknowns" is a key way that practitioners can help to make bad situations a bit more bearable. They can help "set the tone" and provide managers and supervisors with an over-arching strategy about how to handle difficult messages and situations. This sometimes includes providing them a written script and proposed questions and answers for some particularly difficult and potentially emotionally laden situations.

> *I feel like we're usually the ones who have to think of the softer side of things the impact on employees, how to message things ... how to set the stage if it's actually possible so those difficult messages can be heard in the most positive way. And oftentimes I would [personally] deliver that message, but usually I've coached managers or leadership on how to deliver those messages, what words to use, what bullet points to speak to.*

> *I would say HR's role in some of those high emotion situations is to communicate the information effectively to the different stakeholders who are involved in the process ... We have to clearly communicate all of the different aspects of the situation and be prepared to answer any questions that the different stakeholders may have. We're there as a resource to them and sort of as a guide to help them navigate what needs to take place and just be there for them throughout the process.*

> *We must plan for survivors and how to help them deal with their pain too by communicating regularly. We must also deal with the rumor mill as employees lose productivity during times of transition and stress.*

> *We need to understand where trigger points for employees may lie and get ahead of the situation through communication. In this way, we can help to diffuse "hot spots" before they become terribly problematic for people. We are the liaison of those [tough] decisions. We're the "boots on the ground".*

Coach and Advise Managers

A large part of HR's organizational role is to serve both as an advisor to managers and as an implementer of management's decisions; however, they are not usually the final decision-makers. Employees often wrongly think they are and penalize them unfairly as a result.

> *Our role is to serve as consultant, facilitator and coach. However, our resources are limited so we need to coach and train leaders and managers about how to respond to stressful situations too.*

> *Our role often is to advise, not decide. We'll advise on a course of action, we'll advise you of options, we'll make the recommendation but, at the end of the day, if there's going to be a reduction in force, I'm not going to be the one delivering that message. I might be writing the message or coaching the person on how to say the message, but the manager is delivering that message. Then I'm working with employees through the transition with any [severance] packages they may receive or talking about when their benefits are going to end and all those types of questions.*

> *Much of my day is spent in consultation with supervisors who are dealing with difficult employees. I'm advising them about the regulations and what steps we can take, but I'm also like a counselor because they're so frustrated. They're so fed up with this person and they just really need somebody to vent to or somebody to talk to. I try to let them know it's not the end of the world.*

HR practitioners often feel caught between their dual roles of advocating and protecting employees while at the same time supporting their senior leaders and protecting the interests of the organization. They are often involved in situations where there is a need to advocate for and protect employees while challenging management and their proposed response at the same time. This duality of this role creates a great deal of stress and tension for practitioners, leading many to refer to the situation as *a precarious balancing act.*

> *Ours is more a consultative role with the managers and with the executive leadership. We have to ensure that we are protecting the agency while still giving support to the employee as well sometimes giving them information about their appeal rights, and their rights to maintain benefits—all of those kind of issues…*

> *HR is constantly fighting a battle with both employees and management. That causes constant stress, which can create physical illness. Employees get distracted during times of stress. HR has to be there to help them through it. Our role is to be empathetic, but not sympathetic. We need to try to help the employee but, at the same time, we must do the job for the organization.*

HR practitioners are frequently required to deliver bad news to employees, but do not often get to participate in their happier workplace moments (which are most commonly handled by the employee's direct supervisor or manager). As a result, HR is often frustrated by the fact that they are often key contributors to these positive moments, but that their proactive work to make good things happen is often invisible to employees. It is probably safe to presume that if HR was able to more directly deliver positive news to employees, it would likely change their perception about the disproportionate negative role that they tend to take on as toxin handlers.

You've taken on a lot of the emotional stuff that's going on and the good stuff that you do very often you're doing behind the scenes, so you don't get to have the flipside of that where you get to deliver the good news. While you might have created the situation for the good news [a promotion or raise], you're not usually the one who's going to deliver it. That's usually the manager. So, I feel like there's an imbalance where we have all the tough stuff but always don't have the counterbalance of the good stuff.

Five of these core actions of a toxin handler were first identified in the ground-breaking work of Peter Frost (2003, 2004, 2006; Frost & Robinson, 1999). Daniel (2018) extended this earlier work by identifying toxin handling as a central aspect of the role of an HR practitioner and by finding that coaching and advising managers were additional core actions for toxin handlers working in the HR domain (Daniel, 2018). Do any or all of these key roles ring true to your own workplace experience?

References

Daniel, T. A. (2018). *Managing toxic emotions at work: An empirical study of HR's role and its Impact on personal well-being and organizational effectiveness.* https://doi.org/10.13140/RG.2.2.16315.26408.
Daniel, T. A. (2019a, March 6). Viewpoint: HR as toxin handlers. *Society for Human Resource Management HR News.* Retrieved from https://www.shrm.org/resourcesandtools/hr-topics/employee-relations/pages/are-you-a-toxin-handler.aspx.
Daniel, T. A. (2019b, March 13). Viewpoint: How HR can protect itself from toxic emotions. *Society for Human Resource Management HR News.* Retrieved from https://www.shrm.org/resourcesandtools/hr-topics/employee-relations/pages/viewpoint-how-hr-can-protect-itself-from-toxic-emotions.aspx.
Daniel, T. A. (2019c, March 25). Viewpoint: How toxin handlers reduce organizational pain. *Society for Human Resource Management HR News.* Retrieved from

https://www.shrm.org/ResourcesAndTools/hr-topics/employee-relations/Pages/Viewpoint-How-Toxin-Handlers-Reduce-Organizational-Pain.aspx.

Frost, P. J. (2003). *Toxic emotions at work*. Boston: Harvard Business School Press.

Frost, P. J. (2004). Handling toxic emotions: New challenges for leaders and their organizations. *Organizational Dynamics, 33*(2), 111–127.

Frost, P. J. (2006, March/April). Emotions in the workplace and the important role of toxin handlers. *Ivey Business Journal*. Retrieved from https://iveybusinessjournal.com/publication/emotions-in-the-workplace-and-the-important-role-of-toxin-handlers/.

Frost, P. J., & Robinson, S. (1999, July/August). The toxic handler: Organizational hero—and casualty. *Harvard Business Review, 77*(4), 96–106.

7

Why Organizations Need Them

Organizations are constantly changing due to fairly predictable events such as mergers, acquisitions, re-engineering, leadership changes, downsizings, early retirements or due to unprecedented events like those related to the COVID-19 pandemic. The consequence of these events is the creation of intense anxiety and sometimes even paralyzing fear among employees. Some types of pain are one-time (but tumultuous) events created by the sudden departure or loss of a senior leader, a dramatic shift in profitability, or a breach of ethics. Other pain is more chronic, created by policies and programs that systematically generate distress, however unintended (e.g. unreasonable stretch goals, performance or reward systems that cause destructive internal competition, cultures of fear). In addition, chronic toxicity is also the frequent outcome of toxic leaders who generate high levels of emotion and distress among their employees.

By helping employees manage these mostly common but difficult situations, HR enables other employees to stay focused and do their jobs. Without them, the organizational toxicity would continue to build, resulting in higher levels of turnover, increased health costs, more litigation, and reduced levels of employee morale, productivity, and profitability (Daniel, 2018).

> *If you do not have that person who can sit down with people and be compassionate, be a good listener, be a good communicator, I think problems fester, they escalate, and you have huge problems in the end. So, if organizations do have people who are capable of being the toxic handlers, you're going to have a more efficient operation. You're going to have an operation who handles problems at a lower level and they never get out of control. So I think it [having a toxin handler] has a huge impact on an organization.*

It is important work for the organization. It helps employees to be able to manage their workflow and continue being productive when they are not distracted by their personal/professional struggles.

I've had this said to me by the executives I work with that they think that the support that I give them enables them to do their jobs and to be successful in their roles. Therefore, it drives the success of the business.

When people are bitter or sad or frustrated or mad, they are devoting a lot of their energy towards that. I would assume that makes them less productive and less likable to be around ... so having a toxin handler around has to have a positive impact as far as you know allowing people to vent ... so I think it must be a positive if it's handled well.

I believe they have a major impact on organizational effectiveness. Something as small but so important as communication can be the difference between a successful and unsuccessful outcome. Take for example the massive reorganization and downsizing that I was working on. If it's organized, if you bring HR and everybody together before you act, and you make sure to communicate with employees throughout the entire process, making sure that it's transparent and that you are being candid, that's huge.

Because when you're dealing with people's feelings, there is high anxiety and high tension. It's the way those issues are handled and communicated that can be the difference between employees coming to work being unfocused versus being confident that their employers and companies have their best interest at heart.

A happy workforce is an effective workforce. People are happy when they feel supported and they're more effective and/or they work better in teams. If people aren't allowed to bring their personal lives to work or if they feel that there's a line when I walk in that door and I can't bring any of it [their personal lives] with me, you're not getting the best out of that employee.

I kind of think it's a "necessary evil" [referring to the role of a toxin handler]. It presents challenges for the person who serves in that capacity, but it can really help an organization be more effective or efficient, have less turnover and things like that [if the person is successful in a toxin handling role]. I think being able to you come at a situation and help keep it factual, remove emotion from it, and try to get some level of successful outcome can definitely help an organization.

It helps the organization deal with difficult business decisions and minimizes the negative impact of hard decisions on employees. [The toxin handler] in HR limits the negative impact of tough decisions on employees as much as possible.

In addition, because the toxin handler helps to de-escalate emotional situations and make employees feel valued in the process, their work also helps to reduce the potential for lawsuits and claims of discrimination and harassment.

I think if you do not have somebody in the role to respectively deal with it that you get a lot more claims of harassment and discrimination, and maybe potential lawsuits because you don't have the stable calming person who can deescalate and help people move through these issues that they have with one another, and that they have with managers. When you get in the middle of all these investigations and people are not doing the work of the business. They are involved in these lawsuits or investigations because it [the toxic emotion] wasn't dealt with well.

The work protects both employees and the organization. Having HR deal with emotional situations helps get rid of bad employees and helps other employees to feel appreciated and respected by the organization when someone will listen to them and act to assist. The work helps the organization stay in good legal standing and to "stay on the high road" all the time.

The work of an organizational toxin handler is both valuable and important, not only to employees, but also to the organizations where they work. The evidence is unequivocal that organizations need them in order to stay focused and productive (not to mention continuing to be profitable). Given this, it remains somewhat paradoxical that this work is so often undervalued and somewhat invisible.

Reference

Daniel, T. A. (2018). *Managing toxic emotions at work: An empirical study of HR's role and its Impact on personal well-being and organizational effectiveness.* https://doi.org/10.13140/RG.2.2.16315.26408.

8

Friend or Assassin: Whose Side Is HR On, Anyway?

To perform its organizational role responsibly, HR must provide flawless administration services (think employee benefits, compensation, etc.) while also operating as a "strategic partner" to the business. Members of the HR team also advocate for employees and champion organizational change initiatives, while at the same time often being asked to execute difficult human capital decisions made by the senior leadership team (Daniel, 2017).

HR professionals are also called on to explain decisions about policy or the allocation of limited financial resources to employees. Even though they may personally or professionally disagree with the decision, they are the ones who must communicate with employees and "put a good face on it". One HR colleague put it this way (Daniel, 2012):

> *You get worn out and mentally thin from having to take on, manage, guide and resolve issues within the workplace. All this while also maintaining the vision and mission of the organization—which may not always be in line with your own belief system.*

When bad things happen at work to people, they often go straight to HR for help—and most trust that they will get it. Other employees are firmly in the camp of "HR is not my friend" and are suspicious that it is HR who may have been the behind-the-scenes architect of their particular workplace misfortune. This lack of trust leads some to believe that HR acts as an organizational "double agent" or "smiling assassin", pretending to help yet actually being under the control of senior leaders. So, who is right—whose side is HR really on?

In a perfect world, it really should not be an "either/or" proposition. The role of an HR practitioner is to protect the interests of the organization and to also be an advocate for employees. However, expecting an HR practitioner—one with a car loan, a mortgage, and maybe college tuition around the corner—to risk her job to fight against management on behalf of an employee she barely knows is somewhat idealistic—and probably unrealistic for most. This delicate balancing act is what makes the role of an HR practitioner so challenging much of the time.

It is important to remember that the best interests of both "sides" are often really in alignment. Issues that are valuable to performance or employee morale are important to both the business and also to the employees. Issues such as compensation and benefits also involve shared interests. More frequently, though, people come to HR with issues related to their physical or mental health or that of a family member; personal problems that may influence their performance (like divorce or the responsibility of caring for a chronically sick child or an elderly parent); and conflicts with supervisors and co-workers. In these situations, employees generally expect that the information they share will remain confidential.

Many times, it is possible for HR to do that; however, it is also important for employees to realize that HR sometimes may have a legal duty to act on the information and simply cannot maintain the employee's request for confidentiality (e.g. potential criminal violations, mental health issues where violence is threatened, egregious policy violations) (Daniel, 2013a). As a result, it is important to establish clear boundaries with employees from the outset about what HR can (and cannot) realistically do to assist. Doing so will help to set appropriate expectations to avoid any disappointment or surprise.

It is when dealing with performance or an employee's personal issues, however, that workplace situations can get much more challenging. Sometimes, HR must push back on senior leaders and the decision that they may wish to make because it is in the best interests of the business itself (e.g. averting an emotional decision to terminate an employee when the situation does not warrant such extreme action in an effort to avoid a wrongful discharge lawsuit). Hopefully, though, these situations are few and far between.

Why HR Is So Often Misunderstood or Disliked

HR practitioners are called upon to investigate employee complaints, including those related to harassment, abuse, workplace bullying, and similar offenses. If the allegations of misconduct are confirmed, HR generally first confers with legal counsel and then with senior leaders to determine the appropriate consequences for the perpetrator of the offense and how to support the target (Daniel & Metcalf, 2016; Daniel, 2009). The investigative aspect of the role has often caused HR to be perceived as the "internal police" of the organization, a characterization to which most practitioners object and a role which they generally find to be uncomfortable (Fox & Cowan, 2015; Daniel, 2012).

A 2020 global survey of more than 1200 HR practitioners (conducted by New York-based Talent Strategy Group) confirmed these internal tensions, suggesting that "HR is a function at odds with itself". Why? Because some HR leaders see the primary responsibility of the function as helping the company maximize profitability while others see its primary job as helping people grow and develop (Gurchiek, 2020).

Ulrich (1998) acknowledge the paradox inherent in the multiple roles that HR must navigate, especially when it comes to representing the interests of both employee and the organization. He argues that HR professionals "can both represent employee needs *and* implement management agendas, be the voice of the employee *and* the voice of management, act as partner to both employees *and* managers"—but it clearly is not easy to straddle these often-competing roles. It is not surprising, then, that more than half of the HR leaders responding to a survey by a global talent management firm about the complexity of the HR role reported feeling "overwhelmed" and 52% reported that they "did not have the ability to fully cope" with it (SHRM, 2013).

Unfortunately, HR is often perceived by employees as siding with management in some of the worst workplace conflicts and situations brought to their attention. Most of us would probably agree that there is all too often some truth to that perception. The uncomfortable dilemma commonly faced by HR practitioners is aptly stated by Yamada (2013):

> In good and bad workplaces alike, **HR answers to top management**, not to individual employees. Too many well-meaning team players have learned that lesson painfully, thinking that a seemingly empathetic HR manager is a sort of confidante or counselor. There are plenty of good, supportive HR people out there, but ultimately their job is to support the employer's hiring and personnel practices and interests.

Clearly, the role of an HR practitioner is complex. They are often in the unenviable spot of having to straddle the execution of management decisions and initiatives, while at the same time they are also expected to be a sounding board and an advocate for employees.

Fairly or not, HR is often seen as the department that slows things down, generates endless memos, gets into the personal business of employees, holds compulsory trainings, and ruins any "fun" that people may try to have at work. A notorious *Fast Company* cover story by Keith Hammonds (2005) is called *Why We Hate HR*. He laid out a string of damning questions that have resonated throughout American corporations ever since:

> Why are annual performance appraisals so time-consuming—and so routinely useless? Why is HR so often a henchman for the chief financial officer, finding ever-more ingenious ways to cut benefits and hack at payroll? Why do its communications—when we can understand them at all—so often flout reality? Why are so many people processes duplicative and wasteful, creating a forest of paperwork for every minor transaction? And why does HR insist on sameness as a proxy for equality?

A study by Daniel (2013b) identified five key reasons that HR is often negatively perceived by the organization's senior leaders and employees alike. Each of the reasons will be discussed below and supported by actual comments from HR practitioners who participated in the study.

HR Must Often Tell Managers "No"

Managers do not want to be told what to do, and they sure don't want to be told "no". HR is often required to counsel and warn about various actions, and managers are used to being able to make decisions and do what they want to do, when they want to do it. If HR intervenes in that cycle, they don't like it and will often take it out on the HR practitioner involved in the situation.

There is much legality involved in counseling managers and HR must protect both interests (e.g. employees and the company). HR cannot be "yes" men and women. They must be willing to stand their ground when they are right, and challenge management when they are headed off a cliff.

HR must protect the integrity and best interests of the company. Sometimes managers disagree with the recommendations and this is when they will attack the messenger—HR—using HR and staff as a "punching bag"—a place to take out their frustrations.

Organizational Role Is Not Fully Appreciated and/or Understood

HR folks are like police and firemen; cops get grief when they write you a ticket (e.g. quote FLSA to you) but are your best friend when they pull you or your family out of a burning building (e.g. hire you or a referral of yours). Real HR people know it's a thankless profession, most wonder why they do it, but none would ever do anything else. HR people understand the "hero to zero" concept. And if they don't, they should pick another profession.

All I hear from HR—most of the time—is what "can't" be done. The truly valuable HR professionals I've known in my career have been the people who approached an issue from what "CAN" be done—the ones who were willing to try to solve a problem rather than the ones reciting a litany or rules and regulations.

HR Is Perceived as Lacking Business Knowledge

HR professionals are often not in tune with the business. To be relevant, HR must be able to understand issues outside of just HR-related topics.

HR must be able to speak two corporate languages—HR and finance. Most do not speak the latter very fluently. We need to learn to speak EBITDA.

Lack of Professional Credentials, Education, or "Organizational Fit"

Unfortunately, a lot of people who hire HR staff think of HR as an administrative function rather than as a profession, so unskilled and unqualified people are often hired into these roles.

Quite often, HR people have on-the-job training, but not a formal education in the discipline. Conversely, you have people with degrees from all over the spectrum that are not necessarily relevant to HR.

It is largely true that in many organizations, administrative staff—who are often not certified HR professionals—often handle the day-to-day transactional work of the department. As a result, managers are often more frequently in contact with these lower-level and often less educated/less credentialed individuals about benefits and pay-related matters giving rise to this negative perception. There is a widespread perception that HR staff members are not generally educated in the discipline of HR, coming instead from other departments but with little experience in the HR field.

Insecure Managers May See Competent HR Professionals as a Threat

Individuals who feel insecure in themselves or their role may see HR professionals as a threat. If you consider the target of a bully—someone who is typically confident and may pose a risk to a less secure person—then it is not surprising that HR would often be a target.

Because HR professionals are used to dealing with tough problems, they are often very assertive in their dealings with senior managers [who don't like it]. This can set up a power struggle that creates a conflict between the two different personalities.

Managers often get HR involved when they need to get themselves out of trouble or need help resolving a problem. They don't like feeling vulnerable in this way, so they sometimes attack HR when they should be grateful for their help.

It's hard to get some managers to see that HR really can be a partner. This is especially true of those who are threatened by the competence of some really good HR practitioners—who often have direct access to senior management.

Some have suggested that HR only has the interest of management in mind and will always side with the company to keep their job. Still others argue that HR is not objective or fair due to their strong desire to curry favor with executive leaders in order to earn a bigger salary or their next promotion.

Strategies to Improve Perceptions Among Employees and Senior Leaders

It is possible to mitigate some of these concerns. Here are some recommended research-based strategies (Daniel, 2013b) that can be employed by HR practitioners in any industry:

Seek Opportunities to Enhance Business Knowledge and Professional Credibility

It would be helpful for HR professionals to accelerate their understanding of the business (e.g. key financial drivers, largest customers, process issues, industry competitors). In recent years, senior leaders have consistently expressed a desire (and expectation) for HR professionals to understand their company's business, as well as the industry in which they work—how the organization makes its money and how the HR department contributes to the organization's financial goals (Mirza, 2011).

In fact, knowledge of the business is consistently the top-ranked HR leadership quality in studies conducted by the Society for Human Resource Management (SHRM, 2009). An increase in business acumen would improve both the credibility and alignment of the HR practitioner with the organization and is an important step to ensure that HR practitioners are not perceived as underperforming or "out of sync" with the business and other managers.

Increase Communication to Address the Inherent Tension Between HR and Other Managers

The prevailing philosophy used by many organizations (and suggested by many researchers) positions the HR professional as a strategic partner to management. This means that HR often does less problem-solving for managers, instead requiring them to handle many people-related issues on their own (Ulrich, 2007). It is no real surprise that tensions have increased as a result of this shift in focus.

To positively impact this situation, it may be helpful for HR professionals to proactively initiate more contact with managers at all levels, educating them about how to handle the most common people issues and processes. Some time ago, Senge (1990) suggested that HR professionals should become coaches and mentors rather than problem solvers. With a focus on coaching and training, managers will be able to more competently handle these responsibilities on their own which should help to reduce the current tensions that exist. Moreover, there is a possibility that both understanding and trust will be enhanced through this more frequent exchange of expertise, making it a win-win partnership for both parties.

Shift from Role as "Internal Police" to Strategic Business Partner/Compliance Coach

Frequent tensions also arise between HR practitioners and managers due to HR's role in many organizations as the "rule enforcer" (Janove, 2011). This role requires HR to counsel and advise managers who may hold a higher rank about issues related to employee discipline, leave, and other policy-related topics. During these interactions, HR practitioners often are required to take a position that is contrary to the one desired by the manager in order to help protect the company from litigation and minimize risk. Though such interactions are not intended to be personal, they can lead to interpersonal conflict and a perception that HR often says "no" (Mirza, 2011).

To address this tension, it may be helpful for HR professionals to make a shift in role—moving from acting as the "internal police" to one of valued business partner and "compliance coach" (Janove, 2011). To do this, it may be useful for practitioners to provide various alternatives with a corresponding assessment of the risk related to each choice. After discussing the possible options, an informed decision to act can be made based on the facts of the situation and perceived risk. This strategy better aligns HR as part of the team—jointly helping managers to solve problems—rather than as a business outsider who only understands a single aspect of a complex situation.

In human resources, there is no way to avoid the "human" factor. As a result, it is impossible to completely eliminate misunderstandings, conflict, and disappointment among employees. But when HR practitioners consistently set expectations, build and maintain trust, and set clear boundaries, there are bound to be fewer opportunities for tension and conflict. That can only be a good thing for employees, for the business, and for the HR professionals who support them both.

References

Daniel, T. A. (2009). *"Tough boss" or workplace bully: A grounded theory study of insights from human resource professionals.* Doctoral dissertation, Fielding Graduate University. Retrieved from http://gradworks.umi.com/33/50/3350585.html.

Daniel, T. A. (2012, Spring). Caught in the crossfire: When HR practitioners become targets of bullying. *Employment Relations Today, 39*(1), 9–16.

Daniel, T. A. (2013a, Summer). Executive success and the increased potential for ethical failure. *SHRM Legal Report*. Alexandria, VA: SHRM. Retrieved from http://www.shrm.org/publications/pages/default.aspx.

Daniel, T. A. (2013b). Executive perceptions about the effectiveness of HR. *Employment Relations Today, 40*(2), 1–11.

Daniel, T. A. (2017, Winter). Managing toxic emotions at work: An examination of HR's unique role as the "organizational shock absorber". *Employment Relations Today, 43*(4), 13–19.

Daniel, T. A., & Metcalf, G. S. (2016). *Stop bullying at work: Strategies and tools for HR, legal & risk management professionals*. Alexandria, VA: SHRM Books.

Fox, S., & Cowan, R. L. (2015). Revision of the workplace bullying checklist: The importance of human resource management's role in defining and addressing workplace bullying. *Human Resource Management Journal, 25*(1), 116–130.

Gurchiek, K. (2020, February 28). *Is your HR department focused on people or profit?* Society for Human Resource Management. Retrieved from https://www.shrm.org/resourcesandtools/hr-topics/organizational-and-employee-development/pages/is-hrs-focus-on-the-people-or-the-business.aspx.

Hammonds, K. H. (2005, August 1). Why we hate HR. *Fast Company*. Retrieved from https://www.fastcompany.com/53319/why-we-hate-hr.

Janove, J. (2011, August). Become a compliance coach. *HR Magazine, 56*(8). Retrieved from http://www.shrm.org/Publications/hrmagazine/EditorialContent/2011/0811/Pages/0811legal.aspx.

Mirza, B. (2011). Company leaders tell HR: Know the business and be relevant. Retrieved from http://www.shrm.org/hrdisciplines/businessleadership/articles/Pages/BeRelevant.aspx.

Senge, P. M. (1990). *The fifth discipline: The art and practice of the learning organization*. New York: Doubleday.

Society for Human Resource Management. (2009). SHRM ranks leadership qualities for HR professionals. Retrieved from www.shrm.org/about/pressroom/PressReleases/Pages/SHRMRanksLeadershipQualities.aspx.

Society for Human Resource Management. (2013, May). Workplace Forecast. Retrieved from https://www.shrm.org/ResourcesAndTools/hr-topics/behavioral-competencies/Documents/13-0146%20workplace_forecast_full_fnl.pdf.

Ulrich, D. (1998). *Measuring human resources: An overview of practice and a prescription for results*. https://doi.org/10.1002/(SICI)1099-050X(199723)36:3<303::AID-HRM3>3.0.CO;2-%23.

Ulrich, D. (2007). *Human resource champions: The next agenda for adding value and delivering results*. Boston: Harvard Business School Press.

Yamada, D. C. (2013, April 1). Words rarely heard: "Boss, I think you need to get some help". *Minding the Workplace Blog*. Retrieved from http://newworkplace.wordpress.com/2013/04/page/2/.

9

The Price They Pay

Toxin handlers help employees cope with difficult situations, but the role is dangerous because of the personal risk it poses to their well-being caused by the ongoing exposure to other people's toxic emotions (Daniel, 2018). HR is generally "out front" delivering communications directly with employees. As a result, they are often "the face" of the bad news being communicated to employees on behalf of the organization. Toxin handlers often feel they are being penalized—and sometimes villainized—for decisions that they did not actually make but were simply required to communicate.

> Over time, I think it does take a toll on you. I really feel mentally exhausted when I leave work, just completely mentally drained some days and I have more of those days than not. I think professionally we're seen as "the bad guy". No matter what you're doing, it's hard to come to work every day and know that people think you're the "hatchet lady" … I've had people say to me, once they meet me and get to know me, 'oh you're not evil like they say you are'.

Given that HR professionals often develop strong relationships with employees given their interactions with them over the employment lifecycle—from initial recruitment to retirement—the perception among employees that HR was somehow "to blame" or that they were the ones who were responsible for disruptive organizational decisions affected them deeply. They are often conflicted because they are often unable to counter this perception due to their dual role of needing to support both employees and senior leaders.

We are sometimes powerless to fix some large organizational problems—especially ethical dilemmas. This can be demoralizing and demotivating.

I think the role of HR is always viewed in most of these situations, especially terminations and downsizings, as the 'bad guy'. It doesn't matter why something happens, why someone's terminated, why there's a downsize, a RIF, restructuring, HR is the final processor so [employees feel] it's always their fault regardless of how it happened. In my experience, employees always are like 'well HR didn't do enough to keep me from being terminated' or 'they should have known months before this ever happened that it was coming and done something to keep me from losing my job'.

We take the brunt of the anger or the dissatisfaction with things because people don't really understand that it isn't an HR decision to terminate. We simply give the information, give guidance, ensure that the agency is operating within the regulations, the laws and the guidelines, and advise based on lots of factors. But we then take the brunt of 'HR fired me', 'HR let me go', 'HR reassigned me' .... It really is not like that, but that's the perception.

I think HR takes on the brunt of the complaints, and they are often looked at as 'the enemy', unfortunately. That's been in every organization that I've been in. People take their anger out on them.

Supervisors often attempt to "dump" work on HR practitioners. It is not clear whether this is a manipulative effort to off-load their own duties (taking advantage of HR's helping nature) or whether supervisors simply dislike conflict or lack the skills needed to have difficult conversations. In any event, practitioners often need to "push back" against supervisors to make them to do their own work.

Saying "no" to supervisors sometimes causes HR practitioners to feel "guilty" about not helping, but they also know that it is necessary to draw clear boundaries so that they do not inadvertently become the "sounding board" to everyone about everything. In addition, setting boundaries ensures that their willingness to help is not taken advantage of. This issue with supervisors occurs with frequency and is the source of significant stress for HR practitioners.

I think the biggest impact is the struggle to extricate yourself from the blurring of the responsibilities and shifting the workload back to the supervisor—that's the biggest struggle. Over time, it degrades your health.

Managers just don't like the messy people stuff. However, they are paid to manage people. But they really want someone who is good at it or doesn't shy away from the emotional aspects to help them work through these people issues [and that is typically HR].

HR is the only department where supervisors can move a large portion of their organic workload ... they can passively move, either by inaction or by not being very well educated in what their responsibilities really are, their workload onto HR practitioners and [try to] manipulate HR practitioners into doing more than what they are really supposed to be doing.

When a manager doesn't necessarily want to enforce a policy or deal with an employee about a difficult situation, they will often just say to the employee "just call HR and talk to them about it".

In addition, employees often show up in HR's office to present a problem that they have not first talked over or tried to resolve with their supervisor. As a result, HR frequently has to re-direct employees back to their supervisor when they "jump the gun" and seek HR's help first. This causes many to experience feelings of guilt for not helping, but they also know that it is necessary to observe the appropriate chain-of-command and for employees to learn to resolve their own conflicts whenever possible. Similar to the situation experienced with supervisors, HR also frequently needs to "push back" against employees and this also causes significant stress for practitioners.

I've had issues where people came right to me and I said, 'have you talked to your supervisor or manager' and they said, 'no'. Then I said 'well I would like you to go back and do that. I would like you to talk to your supervisor or manager and then come back and see me in HR'. But if you don't have that [chain of command] in place, you're going to have everybody running to HR over everything and they [the HR practitioners] cannot handle that.

Given all of this organizational toxicity and these role-related tensions, it is not surprising, then, that HR professionals are at serious risk for emotional exhaustion, burnout, and withdrawal—both psychological and professional. This can lead to decreased commitment and higher turnover rates.

Practitioners report experiencing significant physical and emotional exhaustion, sadness, anger, stress, lack of sleep, and burnout as a result of their toxin handling role. They also report that it creates a negative impact on their personal relationships and home life. Some of them even seek counseling due to the excessive strain.

I ended up having to have medical testing done because the anxiety was so high. I attempted ways to alleviate some of that, but the bottom line was I still wanted to be able to be the one to help. So, personally and professionally, it [creates] just a lot more stress.

*I found it to be mentally, emotionally draining ... when you come home from work you feel like you're tapped out. Obviously when you have a family, your spouse and your children still have some needs too. I know that when I'm dealing with human capital that we're not dealing with just machines, so it's hard for me to just turn that off. You're constantly thinking about it and about what you can do to help, if anything. You're the middle person and you're not leadership or management in control of solutions or decisions, so it can even become more draining and frustrating because your actions are limited in terms of what you **can** do versus what you **want** to do.*

It can definitely lead to burnout and it can easily lead to some stress in the individual's personal life. I know I spent time at one organization ... after two years of laying people off, it wears on you and you have to move on from it and look to do something else. It can definitely wear on you and burn you out in your professional life—and it can also wear on you in your personal life as well. [Being in HR] is almost like the role of a psychiatrist or a psychologist and you can wear out, burn out from hearing and dealing with so much negativity.

I think we [in HR] tend to take things on and it can beat down our souls ... It bothers us as HR professionals when we are not able to provide those satisfactory outcomes for everyone, so it takes a toll on people personally.

Employees and management both sometimes scream and HR must "take it" from all sides; therefore, an HR practitioner has to find a way to fix himself.

At some point you have nothing left to give. I mean, they just simply suck the life out of you.

Heart attacks and strokes, while rare, can also be complications from the personal distress caused by having to deal with toxic emotions at work. While these more serious medical issues do not occur often, regular exposure to organizational toxicity definitely impacts HR's personal well-being—at least some of the time.

I think the larger an organization is, the volume of what you get can be emotionally draining. So there are a lot more issues that come up with people. By the end of the week, you need to just step away from it and recharge over the weekend and then build yourself back up to start again on Monday morning all over again. I think these toxic emotions, if they come at you in large volume, can almost drain you more than physical work.

Paradoxically, constant exposure to toxic emotions also has the potential to make the toxin handler toxic as he can begin to incorporate the negative emotions into his worldview. As the practitioner begins to view the organization in a more negative light, this can start to create a negative slide in their own performance and morale.

> *I think continual exposure can impact a person to where they're having emotional or physical problems. You see it as burnout or sometimes I think it impacts the person to the point that they [the toxin handler] begin to personally become toxic or negative and they start seeing the organization differently.*

The stress created by constant exposure can also lead to bad habits when it comes to personal decisions related to eating and drinking.

> *I joke about it all the time that I hate my feelings. I know that when I get very stressed at work or I feel like I've absorbed all of other people's crap, I will eat chocolate or go get French Fries because that's how I deal with my feelings of being overwhelmed. Or, after a particularly bad day, I might have a glass—or a bottle—of wine. I'm not going to lie. I joke with people that you're not really an HR practitioner if you're not a drinker, because otherwise you can't get through it.*

Importantly, the stress and emotional exhaustion can take a toll on even the most "gung-ho" HR practitioners, forcing them to leave their organization—and sometimes even the HR profession—altogether.

> *People that are on the receiving end of the information that you're communicating they can react very angrily, they can react and speak to you in a very disrespectful way. After a while, I didn't feel as professional anymore. I didn't feel like I was in a professional environment. I felt like it degraded me from a professional standpoint … so I moved on to a different functional area. So I think professionally it can cause people to change jobs.*

> *Personally [the role] put me in a really bad place. When I thought about work, I thought about it negatively. I thought about work outside of work. On Sunday, whenever it was time to go to work on Monday morning, I would start thinking about it on Sunday at noon and already start dreading it. I didn't want to go there 24 hours later because I could anticipate what these interactions were going to be like the next day. It was so stressful. My personal life suffered, my personal relationships outside of work suffered, so it caused me to seek out other professional opportunities. At that point, it just reached a breaking point where my desire to help others and do the right thing was being outweighed by the stress it was causing me as a person and as a professional. So I had to make a change.*

Most individuals who counsel and advise people about emotional issues have had some form of professional training to give them the skills needed to do this difficult work. For HR practitioners, though, these duties are typically just an incidental part of their "real" job. The result is that they typically lack the training needed to protect their own well-being when counseling employees about high-stress situations where they were experiencing intense feelings.

> *I think if you're a good HR professional you have some level of empath in you where you absorb the emotion. It was really hard from me not to get emotional as I'm trying to speak with her. It was really hard for me to not cry with her.*

The situation is a bit different, though, when it comes to OD and coaching practitioners. They typically have had at least some level of training that may enable them to better handle the effects of trauma and emotional contagion at work.

It is paradoxical, isn't it, that the skills and personality characteristics that draw us to the profession and provide the most benefit and comfort to employees (while positively benefiting our organizations) are the very ones that can harm our own personal sense of well-being if we are not careful to protect ourselves?

Reference

Daniel, T. A. (2018). *Managing toxic emotions at work: An empirical study of HR's role and its impact on personal well-being and organizational effectiveness.* https://doi.org/10.13140/RG.2.2.16315.26408.

10

Running on Empty: Warning Signs of Compassion Fatigue and Burnout

As I hope each of you have personally experienced by now (or soon will), the role of an HR practitioner can be an immensely rewarding experience, and the daily contact with employees and managers—working out problems, resolving conflict, and addressing employee concerns and complaints—is what keeps many of us working in this field. It is a highly specialized type of work that requires emotional sensitivity, patience, listening, and understanding—all hallmarks of high emotional intelligence.

To be effective requires us to open our hearts and minds to employees with whom we work but, over time, the role can also exact a personal toll. HR professionals tend to be empathetic and compassionate, but it is those very qualities that make us vulnerable to being profoundly affected (and even possibly damaged) by our work.

It is true that for many of us, the HR profession is a "calling"; however, as I suspect you will agree, it is not always a bed of roses. The reality is that working in our field can also look like this: increasingly stressful work environments, heavy workloads, scarce resources, cynicism and negativity from co-workers, and sometimes low job satisfaction as a result of feeling like we are drowning in work and just never able to catch up (Moss, 2020).

The result of that cumulative stress can result in feelings of "emptiness" and a broad array of other debilitating psychological conditions, including compassion fatigue, burnout, or both. It is helpful to understand the indicators of these conditions so that you can timely seek counseling or other medical treatment before the symptoms have become so severe that they impact us personally and, by extension, our organizations.

Compassion Fatigue

What Is Compassion Fatigue?

Compassion fatigue has been described as the "cost of caring" for others in emotional and physical pain (Figley, 1982). Figley (1995), one of the earliest and most prominent researchers in the field, explains it further as follows:

> We have not been directly exposed to the trauma scene, but we hear the story told with such intensity, or we hear similar stories so often, or we have the gift and curse of extreme empathy and we suffer. We feel the feelings of our clients. We experience their fears. We dream their dreams. Eventually, we lose a certain spark of optimism, humor and hope. We tire. We aren't sick, but we aren't ourselves.

It is the cumulative emotional residue or strain of exposure to working with those suffering from the consequences of traumatic events (American Institute of Stress, n.d.; Figley, 2002) and is sometimes called "vicarious traumatization" or secondary trauma (Figley, 1995).

Compassion fatigue is characterized by deep physical and emotional exhaustion and a pronounced change in one's ability to feel empathy for those they are helping, and even their loved ones and their co-workers. It is marked by increased cynicism at work, a loss of enjoyment of one's career, and it can eventually transform into depression, secondary traumatic stress, and stress-related illnesses. The most insidious aspect of compassion fatigue is that it attacks the very core of what brings most HR professionals into this line of work—our empathy and compassion for others.

Who Does It Affect?

Compassion fatigue is an occupational hazard, which means that almost everyone who cares about those they are trying to help will eventually develop a certain amount of it, with varying degrees of severity. Compassion fatigue profoundly affects nurses and other helping professionals, including child protection workers, law enforcement, counselors, and prison guards—and it affects HR professionals as well. Clearly the role of organizational toxin handler puts us squarely in the middle of some highly stressful and highly emotional situations and it is hard not to soak up much of the toxins present during the process of trying to help an employee in distress (Daniel, 2018).

Signs and Symptoms of Compassion Fatigue

Each individual will have their own indicators that signal they are moving into the danger zone of compassion fatigue, but here are some of the most common signs and symptoms (Figley, 1982):

- Exhaustion (both emotional and physical)
- Reduced ability to feel sympathy and empathy
- Anger and irritability
- Increased use of alcohol and/or drugs, or both
- Dread of working with certain employees
- Diminished sense of enjoyment of career
- Disruption to world view
- Heightened anxiety or irrational fears
- Intrusive imagery or dissociation
- Hypersensitivity (or insensitivity) to emotional situations
- Difficulty separating work life from personal life
- Absenteeism—missing work, taking many sick days
- Impaired ability to make decisions and care for employees
- Problems with intimacy and in personal relationships

Compassion fatigue exists on a continuum, meaning that at various times in our careers, we may be more immune to its damaging effects while at other times feel very beaten down by it and unable to effectively do our work. Within an organization, there will be, at any one time, some HR practitioners who are feeling fulfilled by their work, many people feeling some of the symptoms, and a few people feeling like there is no other answer available to them but to leave the organization—or worse yet, the profession altogether.

Burnout

Burnout is a psychological syndrome caused by long-term involvement in emotionally demanding situations. It emerges as a response to prolonged, chronic interpersonal stressors on the job (Bratis et al., 2009). It can be distinguished from compassion fatigue in that it is due to workload and institutional stress, not trauma (American Institute of Stress, n.d.).

The World Health Organization (WHO) included burnout in its International Classification of Diseases in 2019. This action made it clear that burnout is a workplace problem—*not* an employee problem or a medical condition.

WHO (2019) defines burnout like this:

Burn-out is a syndrome conceptualized as resulting from chronic workplace stress that has not been successfully managed. It is characterized by three dimensions:

- Feelings of energy depletion or exhaustion
- Increased mental distance from one's job, or feelings of negativism or cynicism related to one's job
- Reduced professional efficacy

This definition is consistent with the way the condition was earlier described by Maslach and Leiter (2017). WHO is careful to point out that burnout refers specifically to phenomena in the occupational context and should not be applied to describe experiences in other areas of life.

Although burnout has become "just part of the job" for many employees, the cost of burnout is substantial. According to the Gallup organization, burned out employees are 63% more likely to take a sick day, and 2.6 times as likely to be actively seeking a different job. Should they elect to stay, they typically have a 13% lower confidence in their performance and are half as likely to discuss how to approach performance goals with their manager (Wigert & Agrawal, 2018). Not surprisingly, they are 23% more likely to visit the emergency room than other employees.

Researchers at the Gallup organization (Wigert & Agrawal, 2018), a well-respected research and survey firm, have concluded that the top five reasons for burnout include:

- Unfair treatment at work (including bias, favoritism, mistreatment by a manager or co-worker, unfair compensation, and/or unfair corporate policies)
- Unmanageable workload

- Lack of role clarity
- Lack of communication and support from the manager
- Unreasonable time pressure

In terms of outcomes, burnout has been frequently associated with various forms of negative reactions and job withdrawal, including job dissatisfaction, low organizational commitment, detachment, a sense of powerlessness, lack of hope, absenteeism, intention to leave the job, and turnover (Schaufeli & Enzmann, 1998). In addition, some physical symptoms are common: headaches, irritability, sleep problems gastrointestinal issues, chronic fatigue, muscle aches, high blood pressure, frequent colds, sudden weight gain or loss (Maslach & Leiter, 1997).

People who are experiencing burnout can have a negative impact on their colleagues, both by causing greater personal conflict and by disrupting job tasks. The research suggests that burnout can be "contagious" and perpetuate itself through social interactions on the job (Bakker, LeBlanc, & Schaufeli, 2005). It can also affect one's family members.

There are ways to cope with feelings of burnout, many of which have been adapted from other work done on stress, coping, and health. Maslach and Goldberg (1998) reported that the most common ways to recover from burnout include:

- *changing work patterns* (e.g. working less, taking more breaks, avoiding overtime work, balancing work with the rest of one's life)
- *developing coping skills* (e.g., cognitive restructuring, conflict resolution, time management)
- *obtaining social support* (both from colleagues and family)
- *utilizing relaxation strategies*
- *promoting good health and fitness*
- *developing a better understanding of one's self* (via counseling or therapy)

Initiatives to moderate workload demands complemented by improvements in recovery strategies through better sleep, exercise, and nutrition can have a direct impact on the exhaustion component of burnout. Cynicism can be reduced by encouraging more recognition from colleagues and leaders within the organization or the individual's profession. In addition, making changes in how they do their job (a process known as "job crafting") has also been found to have a positive impact.

Commonalities and Differences Between Burnout and Compassion Fatigue

Commonalities

The American Institute of Stress (n.d.) suggests that the similarities between the two problems include:

- Emotional exhaustion
- Reduced sense of personal accomplishment or meaning in work
- Mental exhaustion
- Decreased interactions with others (isolation)
- Depersonalization (symptoms are disconnected from real causes)
- Physical exhaustion

Differences

A key difference is that compassion fatigue has a more rapid onset and is usually more pervasive than burnout (which emerges over a longer period of time). Some researchers have suggested that compassion fatigue is, in fact, a type of burnout (Portnoy, 2011). Researchers have demonstrated the impact of these issues on caregiving professionals (as well as the workplace) in terms of decreased productivity, more sick days used, and higher turnover (Potter et al., 2010).

Another key difference from compassion fatigue is that burnout does not necessarily mean that one's view of the world has been damaged nor does it signal a loss of the ability to feel compassion for others.

The *Maslach Burnout Inventory* is an assessment instrument which may be useful if you believe that you or an employee is experiencing burnout (Bria, Spanu, Baban, & Dumitrascu, 2014). It is a validated survey instrument across professional roles, gender, age, and organizational tenure.

Strategies to Avoid These Problems

When HR professionals are overtaxed by the nature of their work, they begin to show symptoms that may be very similar to the toxic emotions being experienced by those whom they are trying to help. Research shows that "who you work for" is one of the biggest determinants of employee wellness. If you work for a supportive manager, your chances of compassion fatigue or burnout are much less likely than if you report to an abusive and controlling one.

It is important to maintain a strong social support network, both at home and at work, so that you have a group of trusted individuals in your life who you can call when you need to talk. You might also want to journal about your workday in order to increase your self-awareness so that you stay in tune with your emotions and have a sense about when you are going into "overload" mode. Regular self-care—through meditation, regular exercise, eating well, not drinking or smoking too much, and so on—can be the most proactive way to avoid these problems.

The American Institute of Stress (n.d.) has provided some recommendations for managing the problem. They suggest that suffering individuals find someone to talk to, understand that the pain one is feeling is "normal", exercise and eat properly, get enough sleep, take some time off, develop outside interests, and identify what is important. Conversely, they recommend that those who suffer should *not*: blame others, look for a new job, buy a new car, get a divorce or have an affair, fall into the habit of complaining with colleagues, hire a lawyer, work harder and longer, self-medicate, or neglect one's own needs and interests.

Remember that compassion fatigue is a process that develops over time, and so is healing from its effects. If you have personally been affected by this workplace-created problem, be patient with yourself and know that, in time, it is possible for you to make a full recovery. If you're lucky, what is needed to recharge your sense of optimism may be as simple as a long weekend at the beach, going camping, or taking a hike in the mountains. Some people might have more success in recharging if they get a massage or spend some quality time with their children or grandchildren.

But the bottom line is this: to care for others, we must also take time to care for ourselves and we do this by putting our own health and wellness at the top of our priority list. That way, we can continue doing what we do best—and that is solving problems and caring for others.

References

American Institute of Stress. (n.d.). Retrieved from https://www.stress.org/.
Bakker, A. B., LeBlanc, P. M., & Schaufeli, W. B. (2005). Burnout contagion among intensive care nurses. *Journal of Advanced Nursing, 51*, 276–287.

Bratis, D., Tselebis, A., Sikaras, C., et al. (2009). Alexithymia and its association with burnout, depression and family support among Greek nursing staff. *Human Resources for Health, 7*, 72–75.

Bria, M., Spanu, F., Baban, A., & Dumitrascu, D. L. (2014). Maslach burnout inventory—General survey: Factorial validity and invariance among Romanian healthcare professionals. *Burnout Research, 1*(3), 103–111.

Daniel, T. A. (2018). *Managing toxic emotions at work: An empirical study of HR's role and its Impact on personal well-being and organizational effectiveness.* https://doi.org/10.13140/RG.2.2.16315.26408.

Figley, C. R. (1982, March). *Traumatization and comfort: Close relationships may be hazardous to your health.* Keynote presentation, Families and close relationships: Individuals in social interaction, Texas Tech University. Retrieved from https://www.researchgate.net/publication/282661160_Traumatization_and_comfort_Close_relationships_may_be_hazardous_to_your_health.

Figley, C. R. (Ed.). (1995). *Brunner/Mazel psychological stress series, No. 23. Compassion fatigue: Coping with secondary traumatic stress disorder in those who treat the traumatized.* Philadelphia, PA: Brunner/Mazel.

Figley, C. R. (2002). *Treating compassion fatigue.* New York: Brunner-Routledge.

Maslach, C., & Goldberg, J. (1998). Prevention of burnout: New perspectives. *Applied and Preventive Psychology, 7*, 63–74. https://doi.org/10.1016/S0962-1849(98)80022-X

Maslach, C., & Leiter, M. P. (2017). *The truth about burnout: How organizations cause personal stress and what to do about it.* San Francisco: Jossey-Bass.

Moss, J. (2020, February 21). Viewpoint: Rethinking workplace burnout. Society for Human Resources Management's *HR Daily.* Retrieved from https://www.shrm.org/ResourcesAndTools/hr-topics/employee-relations/Pages/Viewpoint-Rethinking-Workplace-Burnout.aspx.

Portnoy, D. (2011, July/August). Burnout and compassion fatigue: Watch for the signs. *Health Progress, 92*, 46–50.

Potter, P., Deschields, T., Divanbeigi, J., Berger, J., Cipriano, D., Norris, L., & Olsen, S. (2010, October 14). Compassion fatigue and burnout: Prevalence among oncology nurses. *Clinical Journal of Oncology Nursing, 5*, 56–62.

Schaufeli, W. B., & Enzmann, D. (1998). *The burnout companion to study and practice: A critical analysis.* London: Taylor & Francis.

Wigert, B., & Agrawal, S. (2018, July 12). Employee burnout, Part 1: The 5 main causes. *Gallup.* Retrieved from https://www.gallup.com/workplace/237059/employee-burnout-part-main-causes.aspx.

World Health Organization. (2019, May 28). *Burn-out an "occupational phenomenon": International classification of diseases.* Retrieved from https://www.who.int/mental_health/evidence/burn-out/en/.

Additional Resources

Information and articles for post-traumatic stress syndrome survivors and their caregivers. www.giftfromwithin.org.

Information for caregivers. www.compassionfatigue.org.

Professional quality of life information, including resources to deal with compassion fatigue and burnout, plus the Professional Quality of Life self-test to assess current symptoms. www.proqol.org.

Self-care quiz, articles. www.myselfcare.org.

The American Institute of Stress has a broad array of resources available (e.g. research, articles, DVDs, etc.) on the topic of stress and its related disorders. https://www.stress.org/.

11

Perceived Low Value of HR's Work to Senior Leaders (and How HR Can Fix This)

Most HR practitioners are pretty confident that their toxin handling activities, though important, are invisible to senior leaders. In fact, three-quarters of the participants (73.1%) in the foundational study preceding this book (Daniel, 2018) reported that they did not believe that toxin handling work was recognized or appreciated by senior leaders in their organizations—at all.

Toxin Handling Work Is Not Only Not Appreciated—In Fact, It Is Invisible

HR professionals are overwhelmingly of the opinion that their senior management does not understand what they do to assist employees stay productive, nor are they aware of the positive impact that the work has on organizational outcomes. Practitioners reason (or rationalize perhaps) that this was probably because this work with troubled employees is conducted behind closed doors and kept confidential to protect the employee's privacy. As a result, it seems to be true that this work is virtually invisible to most other people within the organization, including senior leaders (Daniel, 2018).

> I think they sometimes see us as a "necessary evil." They don't always perceive that we contribute to the bottom line by keeping people engaged and helping them through emotional distress.

> I don't think they really understand the work. I don't think they appreciate the work so much as they want results.

> *[I think they sometimes see] us as a "necessary evil." They don't always perceive that we contribute to the bottom line by keeping people engaged and helping them through emotional distress.*
>
> *I think they appreciate it if they get a "yes" or they appreciate it if you solve the problem for them. If it doesn't fall into one of those two categories, it's [considered to be] annoying and definitely not on their agenda to deal with.*
>
> *I don't think they really appreciate it. "That's HR's business" is their answer, "give it to HR" like the old cartoon "give it to Mikey". Let them handle it.*
>
> *Based on my own experience I don't think that they understand the frequency with which it [toxic emotions] gets handled.*
>
> *I just don't think they appreciate it. I think they just assume it's part of the job, like "hey this is your job, you have to deal with it".*
>
> *If you're dealing with people that either are too busy or feel that it [toxin handling] is not important or just don't recognize it as real issue, then I have felt looked down upon for doing that for people—for talking to them and spending the extra time.*
>
> *I don't think they appreciate the work. I don't think that they understand what goes into having those conversations and how much research and effort goes into making just one phone call to communicate one piece of news and walking that one employee through the next steps and answering their questions. I don't think they appreciate it at all or have any idea of how much effort goes into handling even just one situation.*

Some lucky practitioners do feel that their toxin handling work is appreciated and valued, but that view was definitely in the minority.

> *I think when you have good and strong leadership it's appreciated, but that's not always the norm.*
>
> *In my experience, they did appreciate it and probably pushed too much off on HR, especially senior managers, because they didn't always want to deal with anything like that so [their thinking was] "push off to HR".*
>
> *Senior leaders often have to make difficult business decisions to meet strategic objectives. HR helps to minimize the negative impact of those decisions on employees. Management understands the role and values it.*

One of the suggestions offered to ensure that senior leaders really understood and appreciated the value of their toxin handling work was offered wryly:

They should come and work in HR for a couple of weeks …new people who come here are like "wow. I had no idea" [of the complexity and emotion that HR practitioners deal with on a regular basis]. Once people start to realize the parameters that you have to operate in and the actual workload, plus the level of time that has to be spent with some people … right away some people will determine that it [working in HR] is not for them.

Imagine how quickly things would change if this exchange of roles were actually to occur, if only for an hour!

Perceived Low Value of HR's Work to Senior Leaders (and How HR Can Fix This)

Spoiler alert: not only do senior leaders not necessarily understand or respect HR's role in helping to manage organizational toxicity, they also do not seem to fully understand or value HR's contributions to the success of their business in general. To test this theory, a research study examined how 18 senior leaders in organizations throughout North America perceive the effectiveness of HR professionals (Daniel, 2012, 2013). Here are some of the findings that you might find to be of interest:

Strengths of HR Professionals

First, the good news. Senior executives viewed HR professionals as possessing considerable strength in four key areas: (1) education and training of the workforce; (2) mitigation of risk to the organization; (3) providing reliable basic HR services (e.g. compensation, benefits, training); and (4) protecting the interests of both employees and management. This suggests that senior leaders have at least some idea of the contributions that HR makes to the overall success of their business.

Weaknesses of HR Professionals

Conversely, friction points in the relationship were also identified. These include the pervasive perception among senior executives that HR professionals: (1) lack an understanding of business fundamentals; (2) are so focused on administration, rules, and processes that they are impediments to progress; (3) frequently say "no" without suggesting alternative solutions; and (4) are slow to act (or simply fail to respond at all).

Overall Rating

On a scale of 1 to 5 (with 5 being the best and 1 being the worst), the senior leaders participating in the study cumulatively rated the overall effectiveness of the HR function in their organizations at 3.66—roughly translating into perhaps a grade of C+ at best.

At the conclusion of the interview process, HR professionals were subsequently asked to rank order the issues identified by the executives as problematic, with an additional option to select "no issues create increased conflict." Two separate surveys were conducted with a total of 171 HR professionals. These issues were identified as creating the most conflict between senior leaders and HR:

1. Lack of understanding of business fundamentals
2. Concerns that HR is too focused on administrative issues
3. Complaints that HR is slow to act or fails to respond at all
4. Criticism that HR too often says "no" without suggesting alternative solutions

These results clearly demonstrated that HR practitioners have a realistic understanding of the perception of senior leaders about their contributions—as well as their perceived weaknesses.

Six recommendations emerged from the study's findings that can be implemented by HR practitioners to improve their work relationships and organizational impact going forward. They include:

Recommendation #1: Understand the Fundamentals of Business—To Gain Organizational Credibility and Trust
In recent years, senior leaders have consistently expressed a desire—and expectation—for HR professionals to be fully informed about how the organization makes its money, the drivers of cash flow and profits, chief competitors and threats, short- and long-term goals, the trade-offs involved in business decisions, and how the HR department can contribute to the organization's financial goals. It is also critical for HR to be connected to the

human capital-related issues of common concern to executives, such as: *What talent will be the business need in 3–5 years? Where will we find it? How we will grow it?*

This type of knowledge can be obtained both on-the-job and also through conference and training program attendance. Formal HR education and/or professional organizations have not consistently prioritized the development of analytical skills or a depth of knowledge in finance, analytics, technology, and business. However, you undoubtedly already know that business acumen is now one of nine primary competency domains included in SHRM's *HR Competency Model for HR professionals* (SHRM, n.d.). In their own words:

> To really be successful, HR needs to understand the fundamentals of the business with a laser-like focus on the human capital side of the business.
>
> They [HR] need more "street cred" to sit at the big table. They really will not be able to do that until they are more business "savvy" and align their interests with the business needs of the organization.
>
> They need to understand the business that we are in so that they can proactively support us in the things that will make the most difference—recruiting more quickly, developing leadership, and promoting a culture that stimulates engagement among employees.
>
> HR needs to understand the financial aspects of the company and make decisions through a business-oriented framework.
>
> HR is in a role of influence, but they do nothing strategic or proactive. They need more understanding of business issues and strategy.

Recommendation #2: Partner More Closely with Organizational Leaders and Line Managers—To Build Relationships and Connectedness to Positively Support Business Objectives

Senior executives seem to understand that a fully functioning strategic HR function is essential in the current global market. At the same time, however, they also believe that HR is "ineffective and consistently fails to provide value to the organization". To actually become a strategic business partner will require HR to ensure that basic services are executed skillfully and efficiently. It will also require them to expand their knowledge of the business and improve their communication, coaching, and conflict resolution skills in order to interact more effectively with senior leaders.

Making this shift in role will not be easy, but even incremental changes in this direction will likely be met with approval. Importantly, though, if there is a need to remind or tell senior leaders that HR is their "trusted advisor" or "strategic business partner," then the relationship is not quite there yet. Relevant supporting comments follow:

> Move beyond being "nice people who try really hard" to being a strategic and integral partner.
>
> It would be helpful for HR to embrace a new approach/philosophy, such as: "My job is to help you do your job" or "I do not want to slow you down, so let's figure out how to resolve this situation as quickly as possible."
>
> Become less transactional and process-oriented and more strategic and embedded in the business. HR needs to get in sync with the business and help management to find solutions.
>
> HR is not a place for exceptionally bright movers and shakers. It is typically a place for C-level people who have a bachelor's degree and who "like people," but don't really have any other useful skills.
>
> If a bomb went off and they [HR] all went away, no one would miss them or their work.
>
> Line people view staff as impediments to what they want to get done, so they "take runs at HR" because they interfere with the line getting what they want.
>
> HR needs to be proactive in developing relationships with all departments and not just wait until there's a bad situation to deal with. HR is often viewed as the place you go only when there's something bad going on—it's like going to the principal's office.
>
> In the fast-paced changing environment HR can no longer be the "red-headed step-child." They can also no longer be disenfranchised staff employees who provide policies for compliance but not service. We hire the right people in our organization **in spite of** HR, not **because** of them.
>
> We are very clear on what we need, and they seem to work against making good hires ... If HR wants a seat at the table, they need to earn it by providing service to the line departments.

Recommendation #3: Increase the Use of Measurement and Metrics—To Support Evidence-Based Decision-Making and Improve Credibility

Historically HR has not relied on an evidence-based approach to decision-making and forecasting, relying instead on "gut intuition" and/or "doing what is right." While there is no substitute for experience, corporate leaders are increasingly frustrated with the function and its inability to quantify recommendations and present data.

All too often, recommendations are made by HR practitioners with no evidence or analysis to provide support as to why management should consider making those decisions leading some commentators to suggest that perhaps finance should be put in charge of running the function. In some cases, there is simply no evidence to validate what are thought by HR practitioners to be best practices, while in other cases there is evidence to suggest that what are thought to be best practices are actually inferior ones. In short, not enough organizations practice evidence-based human capital management. As a result, HR professionals are often perceived as under-performing and disconnected from the rest of the organization.

We need to bring the same degree of rigor and discipline to the HR function that is commonly found in other functions. An increase in the use of evidence-based decision-making, measurement, analytics and technology, along with improved business acumen will go a long way toward improving HR's organizational credibility—and its actual impact.

Having said that, a word of caution is in order: it is important not to go overboard. We must focus on maintaining a balanced approach so that we do not begin to count and measure everything while losing sight of the organization's most important asset—its human capital.

> HR needs to understand the financial aspects of the company and work through a business-oriented framework. That means more analysis/more measurement and holding themselves to the same rigorous standards that others in the organization are required to meet.
>
> HR is generally working on the wrong things and do not present information analytically or in terms of its impact on the business. As a result, they are considered to be fairly naïve by operating people.
>
> Who would want to go into HR as a profession? If someone says to me that they want to study HR, I immediately think "well, here's a C student."
>
> HR does not seem able to look out in the future and forecast people needs. They need to increase their use of measurement and metrics to help the organization make better human capital decisions.

Recommendation #4: Improve Speed and Access—To Increase Availability, Visibility, and Improve Negative Perceptions of the Function

There is a distinct difference between activity versus impact; in fact, it is possible to spend all of one's time working hard and engaged in activity yet have no organizational or strategic impact at all. HR practitioners often have low visibility and are slow to respond because they are swamped with administrative tasks. Does that sound like your workday?

While many of these tasks come with a sense of urgency, not all of them are really important. Increasing the availability of HR practitioners and accelerating the speed of response would help to overcome a perception that HR is disconnected from the real work of the organization. Slow response times and frequent lack of availability causes organizational frustration and a pervasive sense that HR is not responsive as evidenced by the mountain of comments delivered with emotional intensity on this issue:

> They take **forever** to get anything done—including simple things like the return of phone calls. It is not uncommon for days or weeks to go by without a response.

> They [HR] have trained all of us in the organization not to go to them for help as they are unwilling (or unable) to provide it. Most people try hard to avoid interfacing with HR and simply work around them—if we can do it on our own, we just do in order to get it done. It may be imperfect, but at least we make progress.

> It takes 2–3 tries to get anything done with them. You have to push and cajole them to get them to make a decision or act. HR has set the bar so low that no one wants to deal with them.

> HR tends to feel that they are understaffed, undervalued and misunderstood. What they don't seem to realize is that every staff group feels the same way ... but HR acts "put upon" and as if they are special and should be exempted from the same expectations that other groups must meet in terms of responding quickly, etc.

> HR is an impediment to performance—they do not provide good service and they just get in the way of making progress. HR staff need to be held accountable like everyone else for being responsive and meeting their commitments.

> They are always slow to respond—in our organization, we fondly refer to HR as "the black hole."

> People are negative about HR because they don't really know what HR is doing for the organization. When they don't call back or respond to issues or questions, people begin to think negative thoughts—they become cynical and start saying things like "HR spends all of its time visiting the spa and getting massages (mistakenly)."

> Answer the phone and return emails in a reasonable amount of time (if a quick answer is not possible, at least get back to the person with an estimated time that you will be able to respond).

> Avoid being a "sub organization" that lives and works apart from everyone else. HR is often isolated (both physically and in terms of really being a part of the business) and, as a result, is disconnected. Don't stay locked up in the office—get out and interact more. Be available and accessible!

> HR slows things down (often called "Miss Pokey Pants" by operating people in the organization).

Recommendation #5: Simplify—Ruthlessly Eliminate Unnecessary Paperwork, Processes, Rules, and Policies

A significant amount of time is still being invested in the traditional transactional activities of HR, rather than the transformational ones that have been proven to impact the company's bottom line. World-class companies are working hard to simplify their services by increasing their reliance on technology. Through the implementation of self-service options for payroll, training, total rewards, administration, and staffing services, the premise is that automation and standardization in these areas will lead to higher-quality decision-making and lower costs.

Mundy (2012) offers a useful framework for practitioners to use when evaluating new and existing policies, processes, and programs. He suggests subjecting all decisions to this question before taking action: *does it cause friction in the business or does it create flow?* **Friction** is anything that makes it more difficult for people in critical roles to advance the objectives of the business. **Flow**, on the other hand, is doing everything possible to remove barriers and promote better performance. Some intense comments from senior leaders about the performance of the HR function as a whole:

> *They make me absolutely crazy by their obsession with paper and forms. We are getting "papered to death" by HR. We need HR to have a business orientation—what we don't need is HR that requires multiple forms to get their jobs done. Why can't they just make things happen???*
>
> *At my company, it seems like we need policies and procedures just to go to the bathroom ... so what happens? No one wants to work with HR.*
>
> *We need HR to stop being so rule-oriented and form-driven and actually help plan and manage our human capital needs, run projections, find talent, etc. In fact, human capital drives a significant part of our capital budget, so it is a hugely important function.*
>
> *Work on processes so that they are not so form-intensive or do something to help speed up the process to make it simpler and faster. Increase the use of technology to automate processes and/or push information downstream.*
>
> *Make everyone's job easier—"Loosen up" and minimize the heavy reliance on processes, procedures, rules, and paperwork.*

Recommendation #6: Stop Saying "No"—Provide Multiple Alternatives with an Assessment of the Risk Involved with Each Option

The role of an HR practitioner frequently requires HR to counsel senior managers about complex issues such as employee discipline, policy interpretation, and the like. During these types of interactions, practitioners often must take a position that is contrary to the one desired by the manager in order to help minimize risk and protect the company from litigation. Though such interactions are not intended to be personal, they can lead to interpersonal conflict and a perception of HR as unhelpful because they respond all too often with a flat "no."

To address this tension, a shift in role is recommended. Rather than simply saying "no" or "you can't do that," executives in this study suggested that a better strategy would be for HR practitioners to provide alternatives with a corresponding assessment of the risks related to each choice. Jointly making decisions by providing an array of solutions to help managers solve problems would align HR as a more integral part of the team as evidenced by these comments:

> *Bring solutions, not just problems. This would create a more symbiotic relationship with everyone in the organization—not just management.*
>
> *Provide alternatives with an assessment of the risk involved for each recommendation—then make the decision together after a full discussion of the pros/cons.*
>
> *Be more definitive and provide solid answers. Having said that, everyone thinks that they can do HR, but they can't!*
>
> *Dig deep into issues to provide viable solutions that, even though they may be imperfect, advance the organization's objectives in a timely manner.*

Implications for the HR Profession

While not exactly representing a vote of confidence, these executive insights should not be discounted or ignored simply because they tell us things that we really do not want to hear. These views provide important information that can be used as a basis to target and remedy the perceived weaknesses of our profession so that we can reduce points of conflict, earn the respect of senior leaders, and truly move in the direction of becoming a more valued strategic business partner.

The HR function holds a unique and important organizational position with regard to people and talent. There is no other group better positioned to address the key drivers of organizational success—which most of us would agree include talent, culture, and leadership. However, the study's findings strongly suggest that the HR profession has some very real challenges or, at the very least, a serious perception problem.

Whether or not we believe the criticisms to be fair, these perceptions *are* the reality of senior leaders when it comes to HR—at least for some. There have been countless public criticisms leveled at HR throughout the years (remember that scathing *Fast Company* article titled *Why We Hate HR* that touched a nerve and started it all back in 2005 (Hammonds, 2005)? Then Cappelli (2015) piled on again in a *Harvard Business Review* article a decade later (but, in all fairness, this time there were actually helpful suggestions about what HR can actually do about it). It is reasonable to assume that senior leaders in other organizations may hold similar views (Mirza, 2011).

It is, in my judgment, way past time for HR to stop *asking* for a "seat at the table". Instead, we need to simply *claim* it by making our contribution abundantly clear to the organization—day after day after day—why we should be there.

How will we do this? By taking these recommendations to heart and getting serious about improving our business acumen, sharpening our analytical skills, improving our availability and speed of response, simplifying processes, by partnering more closely with line and corporate leaders, and by taking care to stop our instinctive "no" response and instead offer useful solutions. As noted by Gifford Pinchot (n.d.):

> *The vast possibilities of our great future will become realities only if we make ourselves responsible for that future.*

What if senior leaders actually began to *demand* our presence in key strategy meetings because our views were considered to be that crucial to the decision-making process? That is the future for HR that I hope for—and one that I actually think is possible to achieve. Of course, it is much easier to identify what needs to change than it is to actually make it happen. The COVID-19 pandemic, while tragic in so many ways, has created a bright spotlight on the function. HR professionals everywhere have been stepping up to manage and solve the many unique problems it has created. By all reports, HR is getting rave reviews from both employees and senior leaders alike for their leadership in these unchartered waters. It will be up to each of us to continue to demonstrate our value proposition—and it is significant. Despite the challenges (or maybe because of them), I really don't think there has ever been a better time to be in HR.

References

Cappelli, P. (2015, July/August). Why we love to hate HR ... and what HR can do about it. *Harvard Business Review*. Retrieved from https://hbr.org/2015/07/why-we-love-to-hate-hr-and-what-hr-can-do-about-it.

Daniel, T. A. (2012). LinkedIn Poll: *Which of these criticisms of HR create the most conflict between executives and HR professionals?* Retrieved from http://www.linkedin.com/osview/canvas?_ch_page_id=1&_ch_panel_id=1&_ch_app_id=1900&_applicationId=1900&_ownerId=0&appParams=

Daniel, T. A. (2013). Executive perceptions about the effectiveness of HR. *Employment Relations Today, 40*(2), 1–11.

Daniel, T. A. (2018). *Managing toxic emotions at work: An empirical study of HR's role and its impact on personal well-being and organizational effectiveness.* https://doi.org/10.13140/RG.2.2.16315.26408.

Hammonds, K. H. (2005, August 1). Why we hate HR. *Fast Company*. Retrieved from https://www.fastcompany.com/53319/why-we-hate-hr.

Mirza, B. (2011). *Company leaders tell HR: Know the business and be relevant.* Retrieved from http://www.shrm.org/hrdisciplines/businessleadership/articles/Pages/BeRelevant.aspx.

Mundy, J. C. (2012, July 5). Why HR still isn't a strategic partner. *Harvard Business Review*. Retrieved from http://blogs.hbr.org/cs/2012/07/why_hr_still_isnt_a_strategic_partner.html.

Pinchot, G. (n.d.). *Brainy quotes*. Retrieved from https://www.brainyquote.com/quotes/gifford_pinchot_140386.

Society for Human Resource Management. (n.d.). *SHRM competency model.* Retrieved from https://www.shrm.org/learningandcareer/career/pages/shrm-competency-model.aspx.

12

Promising Macro Strategies to Minimize Harm to Toxin Handlers

Evidence-based ideas to reduce the harm presently occurring to organizational toxin handlers fall into two primary areas: organizational strategies, and larger societal changes which include legal reforms (Daniel, 2018). Some of the most promising strategies will be further discussed in this chapter, and you may be inspired to think of more! If you do, I hope you will follow up and let me know your thoughts.

Organizational strategies will be examined first as they include recommendations over which you probably have the most direct control.

Organizational Strategies

Formalize Toxin Handling Responsibilities

Earlier research has shown that organizations which make handling emotionally charged employee problems a formal part of HR's responsibilities tend to have toxin handlers experiencing lower levels of emotional exhaustion (Kulik, Cregan, Metz, & Brown, 2009). In addition, when this occurs, the HR function is perceived as more effective, even when the handlers are engaged in high levels of toxin handling.

To formalize these duties, organizations should consider including these toxin handling responsibilities in the HR employee's job description, set the goals to be achieved, and monitor and reward their performance during performance reviews. Formalizing this expectation can help reduce the stress that is often created when employees have a somewhat ambiguous organizational role.

Focus on Building a "Culture of Care"

The involvement of senior leadership in building a "culture of care" can help to mitigate the inevitable toxic emotions occurring at work and the need for toxin handlers. If senior leaders demonstrate that they truly care about employees and are honest and ethical in their interactions, some of the organizational toxicity that is bound to exist from time to time will be lessened.

> *Companies like Google or Apple really put their employees and their employees' mental health first. They create an environment of caring for their employees versus environments where there is not a lot of open communication.*
>
> *Support wellness and workouts. Manage better so that there are fewer terminations and force reductions.*
>
> *Let normal attrition take place to avoid severe future impact from reductions in force. Continually improve processes to minimize the need for downsizings and terminations. Engage in long-term thinking. Do things right and be ethical. Pre-plan for predictable business cycles to minimize the impact on the workforce. View employees as a talent issue and not a problem to be solved. This changes the dynamic of the types of decisions that are made. Be proactive.*

Develop an Intentional Partnership Between HR and Senior Leaders

There is consensus among HR professionals that there should be more of an intentional partnership between HR and senior leaders in order to reduce organizational toxicity and make HR feel more valued and supported.

> *Senior leadership should be there for HR, HR should be there for them, and they should both be on the same page.*
>
> *I think there has to be intentional partnership between HR and the management team to make all of this work. If that never happens, I think HR is going to take on the whole burden and that is not fair to the department.*

Expand Employee Communications

Regular and honest communications with employees builds trust. When trust exists, people are more willing to believe that management is making the best decisions possible under the circumstances, even when those decisions have a negative impact on employees. Participants recommended that organizations should strive to share as much information as possible with as much advance notice as is possible in order not to blind-side employees and to allow them to understand why and when certain decisions will be made, and most importantly *why*.

> *Communicate, communicate, communicate. And be honest and have ethics and integrity. Don't lie, cheat, or steal ... Employees have to know that they can trust you because you have ethics and integrity and that what you are telling them is real. If employees believe that, then the organization will get through it [tough times] with the least amount of stress and after-effect.*

> *Take time to communicate with and help employees who are impacted by difficult business decisions. Validate employee feelings and listen—really listen.*

Rotate HR Practitioners

Certain functional areas of HR, especially employee and/or labor relations, tend to create more opportunities for toxin handling. Individuals in these roles should be given the opportunity to rotate through a variety of positions in order to reduce the possibility of emotional exhaustion, stress, and burnout.

> *And they get burnt out. They try to go to the positive side. They try to remain positive, but you have so much stress and you hear so much negative, it is hard to go to the positive side and stay there. So, I think the person who is the toxin handler has a really tough job. I think you get burnt out very quickly. I suggest in HR that there's a rotation of jobs so one person doesn't have to take that job [of toxin handling] and that's all they do.*

Ramp Up Soft Skills Training

Training in stress management, communication skills, and conflict management may also be beneficial in reducing the organizational anxieties and stresses that exist in every organization. Expanding the available "soft skills" training could also help to give other managers and supervisors the competencies needed to share some of this work so that toxin handling situations are not assumed by HR in all cases.

> *A lot of companies do not think there's a need for soft skills training, but I totally disagree with that. I think people need to learn to be good communicators. I need people need to learn to be good listeners. People need to learn to be compassionate. Some people are because it's their personality. Other people need to be told how to do it. So, a company who invests in training their employees on the soft skills will be much better prepared to handle people. And even others [outside of HR] can learn to become a toxin handler.*

Recognize and Appreciate the Work

It is critical for organizations to recognize the importance of the extra-role work of toxin handling performed by HR practitioners. These practitioners, and the compassion they bring to their organizations, are an important reason why companies manage to function in the midst of difficult times. Support from senior leaders—in the form of time and resources, plus recognition and appreciation of the importance of the work—would help to reduce some of the stress associated with this often invisible (but highly time consuming) role on HR practitioners.

> *Acknowledge that it's real and it's needed [toxin handling]. Respect the people who are able to do it, who are capable of doing it, and perform it well.*
>
> *Appreciate the burden that HR is shouldering [for the organization].*
>
> *Show appreciation to HR for acting as a "buffer" or "organizational shock absorber" which allows employees to have a place to vent and then go back to their regular jobs.*

When the role is formalized and the work is recognized and valued, organizations will be more conscious about providing HR with the time, resources, and support required for them to perform these additional duties. In turn, this will help to minimize the negative impact on those who do the work.

Based on a growing body of empirical research, some other recommended strategies to minimize the harm to HR practitioners include:

Develop a Culture of Respect

It is recommended that organizations take steps to move from a *culture of fear* to a *culture of respect* by establishing and maintaining a workplace culture that requires that both respect and dignity be afforded to all employees; that is, a workplace climate where employees feel valued, supported, and where they are encouraged to do their best work (Daniel, 2003a, 2003b). In research released by the Society for Human Resource Management Foundation (SHRM, 2016b, 2016c), the respectful treatment of employees at all levels is the single most important contributor to the overall job satisfaction of employees.

When employees perceive that their organization is fair, respectful, and committed to them, they tend to reciprocate by giving their best effort as well—a concept which has been referred to as *perceived organizational support* (Eisenberger, Huntington, Hutchison, & Sowa, 1986; Wikipedia, n.d.). Moreover, there is research suggesting that organizations which create an ethical infrastructure to support a respectful culture (through the implementation of their policies, conflict management training, formal sanctions, communication, social norms, and conflict management climate) are perceived as more successful in their interventions against a toxic workplace culture (SHRM Foundation, 2016c; Einarsen, Mykletun, Skogstad, Einarsen, & Salin, 2015).

Adopt New Policies and/or Update Existing Ones

Researchers and practitioners have recommended that policies should be adopted or updated to include language that specifically details the type of abusive misconduct that is prohibited (along with examples). In addition, the policy should assure employees that there will be no retaliation for raising an issue and detail the possible consequences for failing to observe these behavioral expectations (e.g. Daniel & Metcalf, 2016; Daniel, 2009a, 2009b, 2009c; Namie & Namie, 2000, 2011; SHRM, 2012; Cowan, 2009, just to name a few).

Including a provision requiring *all* employees to notify management if they see a fellow employee being abused or mistreated will ensure that co-workers who witness a problem feel obligated to speak up and alert the company's management before the situation escalates further (SHRM, 2016a-Behavioral Competency #2-Ethical Practice; American Bar Association, 2012). Given that policies and practices are considered to be contractually enforceable in most jurisdictions, it should be noted that HR will typically work in close partnership with the company's legal counsel in order to navigate the myriad of potential issues with legal implications.

Ensure Periodic Communication and Training About Conduct Expectations

HR can implement and enforce the company's conduct expectations through periodic training and frequent internal communications. It may also be pragmatic—as well as both cost- and time-effective—to incorporate conduct expectations into existing policies and programs (Daniel & Metcalf, 2016; Daniel, 2009a).

Moreover, consistent with recommendations by the EEOC's *Select Task Force on the Study of Harassment in the Workplace* (2016), it is a good idea for companies to offer workplace civility training which focuses on the promotion of respect and civility at work. In addition, teaching bystanders to recognize potentially problematic behaviors can improve the sense of collective responsibility that employees feel and provide the tools and resources that bystanders need to intervene when they witness abusive conduct. When trained properly, witnesses (e.g. supervisors, colleagues, and managers) can be an organization's most important resource in preventing and stopping workplace abuse, thereby reducing the organizational toxicity that these types of incidents typically generate.

Track Key Metrics and Regularly Audit Key Processes

Critical HR processes should be regularly audited, and metrics should be tracked in key areas (e.g. employee complaints, employee discipline, workers' compensation claims, absenteeism, and termination). Regular monitoring of this data can serve as an "early alert" to the organization about potential problems that may be developing within a department or work group (Daniel & Metcalf, 2016; Daniel, 2003a, 2003b, 2009a).

Conduct Periodic Climate Surveys

Employee satisfaction surveys are typically used by organizations to assess the "climate" of the organization—how employees are feeling about key issues related to employee engagement. This data can also serve to alert the company about problems that may be developing; however, action should be taken quickly to address any problems identified by the survey data. Doing so will help to generate trust among employees because they will see that the organization is taking their feedback seriously (Van Rooy & Oehler, 2013).

The Way Forward: A Modest Proposal

My view is that changes need to happen in three key areas in order for us to make any headway in combating the problem of organizational toxicity in American corporations: change to the legal system, the employment relationship, and to the organizational system as a whole. Each of these areas will be discussed next.

Changes to the Legal System

It will be important to take steps to ensure that the risk of punishment for bad behavior and disrespect outweighs its potential rewards (Ford, 2011). It is reasonable to assume that leaders who use abusive tactics are rational human beings who understand the consequences of their actions—and who will not engage in this type of behavior if the perceived risk of doing so is personally too great.

The law cannot require corporations to care about the health and well-being of their employees or simply order everyone to be "nice" to one another (Yamada, 2008, p. 554). However, the law *can* implement legal incentives for employers to act preventively in terms of the mistreatment of employees by mandating training for employees and managers. Through the mandate of sexual harassment protections, it has been clearly demonstrated that the implementation of legal measures can—and does—positively impact the workplace.

I hope you will agree with me that it is time for the United States to follow the lead of many countries throughout the world and develop legal safeguards for those who have been seriously mistreated at work. Although legal intervention is not an ideal solution, it is important to remember that modern organizations came into existence through legislation and judicial decisions dating back to the 1880s (Greider, 2003). That legal framework is important because it forms the template for how things work today, acting like "unforeseen boundary markers between society's aspirations and corporate capitalism's prerogatives" (p. 212).

There is a need to provide relief and compensation to targets of severe workplace abuse who can demonstrate tangible harm. Employers must be required to act preventively and responsibly to prevent abusive mistreatment of individuals at work. In my view, implementation of model legislation that has been proposed in the United States by Professor David Yamada (referred to as the *Healthy Workplace Bill*) would be a brilliant start.

Changes in the law to provide workplace protections for targets of abusive misconduct would provide the initial high-impact leverage point that is likely to create momentum toward larger-scale societal reform. Ironically, the shift to more cooperative and respectful workplaces is also likely to result in organizations being more productive and profitable (Greider, 2009).

Changes to the Employment Relationship

It is also time to re-think the current state of our corporations and the nature of its relationship with employees. Although organizations can no longer provide lifetime employment, they *can* provide an alternative vision of work that provides security and a mutually satisfying relationship for a specific but limited period of time—what has been referred to in the business press as a "tour of duty" (Hoffman, Casnocha, & Yeh, 2013).

Under this approach, the employee would have temporary job security (generally for a two to four-year period) along with training to help advance his or her career. At the conclusion of this period, a decision would be made to determine whether the employee remains with the company for "another tour" or takes a position elsewhere. As noted by Hoffman et al. (2013):

> The key is that it gives employer and employee a clear basis for working together. Both sides agree in advance on the purpose of the relationship, the expected benefits for each, and a planned end.

This type of relationship would arguably engender more trusting relationships in that it gives employees an unambiguous understanding of the mutual commitments involved and establishes a clear timeline for when the parties will discuss whether or not the relationship will continue. This approach is a stark contrast to the current situation where the employee is asked to commit to the organization but the corporation essentially has no obligations in return. The current ambiguity surrounding the employment relationship causes both the employee and the employer to lie (or at least pretend that it is different than it really is), creating fundamental distrust and insecurity on both sides.

The "tour of duty" approach would create a new employment relationship in which the employer-employee obligations are mutual, expectations about the relationship are clearly defined, and employees are treated in an adult and respectful manner (as opposed to the parent-child/master-servant relationship that currently exists). Recruitment, retention, and corporate reputation are also likely to positively increase for those companies who elect to embrace this new approach.

Changes to the Organizational System

In additional to legal reforms and changes to the employment relationship, it will be necessary to consider other critical leverage points—places within a complex organizational system where a small shift in one thing can create big changes in everything (Meadows, 1999, 2008). The problem is that organizational systems are highly resistant to change. As explained by Pirsig (1974):

> To speak of certain government and establishment institutions as "the system" is to speak correctly ... They are sustained by structural relationships even when they have lost all other meaning and purpose. People arrive at a factory and perform a totally meaningless task from eight to five without question because the structure demands that it be that way. There's no villain, no "mean guy" who wants them to live meaningless lives. It's just that the structure—the system—demands it and no one is willing to take on the formidable task of changing the structure just because it is meaningless. (pp. 119–121)

There are several other promising places to intervene, including additional reforms such as:

- Restructuring the fundamental purpose of corporations so that organizations have both a reason and incentives to consider all of their stakeholders, not just institutional investors and activists
- Incorporating measures of civility, empathy, and kindness into our corporate performance evaluation and reward systems so that employees are evaluated and rewarded not only on the results that they achieve, but also on *how* they are achieved

Greider (2003) vividly describes the need to make sweeping fundamental changes to the organizational systems in which most of us work:

In basic character, the corporation resembles a shrewd and muscular wild animal that sooner or later figures out how to break out of its cage. Instead of building new cages, we should investigate the DNA of these creatures. (p. 211)

I couldn't agree more. Incremental change will not impact the systems in which we live, work, and play. We need to completely re-think the purpose of corporations and how we want people to be treated when working for them.

As HR professionals, you can play a key role in leading the charge for this to happen by continuing to advocate that employees be treated with fairness, dignity, and respect at work. Through the development of rational and humane policies, processes, procedures, reward structures, incentive programs, and performance review systems, just to name a few, this strategy can actually be more than a mere slogan or catch phrase. SHRM and the US Chamber of Commerce can also be great allies in this effort, but it will take advocacy and persistence to achieve any real and lasting changes in our workplaces.

References

American Bar Association. (2012). *Model anti-bullying policy*. Retrieved from http://www.americanbar.org/content/dam/aba/events/labor_law/2012/03/national_conference_on_equal_employment_opportunity_law/mw2012eeo_eisenberg2.authcheckdam.pdf.

Cowan, R. L. (2009). *Walking the tightrope: Workplace bullying and the human resource professional*. Doctoral dissertation, Texas A & M University.

Daniel, T. A. (2003a). Tools for building a positive employee relations environment. *Employment Relations Today, 30*(2), 51–64. Retrieved from http://onlinelibrary.wiley.com/doi/10.1002/ert.10086/abstract

Daniel, T. A. (2003b). Developing a "culture of compliance" to prevent sexual harassment. *Employment Relations Today, 30*(3), 33–42. Retrieved from http://onlinelibrary.wiley.com/doi/10.1002/ert.10096/abstract

Daniel, T. A. (2009a). *"Tough boss" or workplace bully: A grounded theory study of insights from human resource professionals*. Doctoral dissertation, Fielding Graduate University. Retrieved from http://gradworks.umi.com/33/50/3350585.html.

Daniel, T. A. (2009b). *Stop bullying at work: Strategies and tools for HR & legal professionals*. Alexandria, VA: SHRM Books. Retrieved from http://shrmstore.shrm.org

Daniel, T. A. (2009c, July 12–17). *Workplace bullying in American organizations: The path from recognition to prohibition*. 53rd Annual Conference of the International Society for the Systems Sciences, The University of Queensland, Brisbane. Retrieved from http://journals.isss.org/index.php/proceedings53rd/article/viewFile/1209/400.

Daniel, T. A. (2018). *Managing toxic emotions at work: An empirical study of HR's role and its impact on personal well-being and organizational effectiveness.* https://doi.org/10.13140/RG.2.2.16315.26408.

Daniel, T. A., & Metcalf, G. S. (2016). *Stop bullying at work: Strategies and tools for HR, legal & risk management professionals.* Alexandria, VA: SHRM Books.

EEOC's *Select Task Force on the Study of Harassment in the Workplace.* (2016). Retrieved from https://www.eeoc.gov/eeoc/task_force/harassment/.

Einarsen, K., Mykletun, R. J., Skogstad, A., Einarsen, S., & Salin, D. (2015, May 24). *Ethical infrastructure in combating unethical behavior in organizations: The case of workplace bullying.* EAWOP Conference, Oslo, Norway.

Eisenberger, R., Huntington, R., Hutchison, S., & Sowa, D. (1986). Perceived organizational support. *Journal of Applied Psychology, 71*(3), 500–507.

Ford, C. (2011, December 11). *Bullying won't end until we stop rewarding it.* Retrieved from http://beaconnews.ca/blog/2011/12/bullying-won%E2%80%99t-end-until-we-stop-rewarding-it/.

Greider, W. (2003). *The soul of capitalism: Opening paths to a moral economy.* New York: Simon & Schuster.

Greider, W. (2009, May 6). *The future of the American dream.* The Nation. Retrieved from http://www.thenation.com/article/future-american-dream.

Healthy Workplace Bill. Retrieved from http://www.healthyworkplacebill.org.

Hoffman, R., Casnocha, B., & Yeh, C. (2013, May 23). Tours of duty: The new employer-employee compact. *Harvard Business Review.* Retrieved from http://hbr.org/2013/06/tours-of-duty-the-new-employer-employee-compact/ar/1.

Kulik, C. T., Cregan, C., Metz, I., & Brown, M. (2009). HR managers as toxin handlers: The buffering effect of formalizing toxin handling responsibilities. *Human Resource Management, 48*(5), 695–716.

Meadows, D. (1999). Leverage points: Places to intervene in a system. *The Sustainability Institute.* Retrieved from http://www.sustainer.org/pubs/Leverage_Points.pdf.

Meadows, D. (2008). *Thinking in systems: A primer.* White River Junction, VT: Chelsea Green Publishing.

Namie, G., & Namie, R. F. (2000, 2003, 2009). *The bully at work: What you can do to stop the hurt and reclaim your dignity on the job.* Naperville, IL: Sourcebooks.

Namie, G., & Namie, R. F. (2011). *The bully-free workplace: Stop jerks, weasels, and snakes from killing your organization.* Hoboken, NJ: Wiley.

Pirsig, R. (1974). *Zen and the art of motorcycle maintenance.* New York: Harper Torch.

Society for Human Resource Management. (2012). *SHRM survey findings: Workplace bullying.* Retrieved from http://www.shrm.org/Research/SurveyFindings/Articles/Pages/WorkplaceBullying.aspx.

Society for Human Resource Management. (2016a). *The SHRM body of competency and knowledge.* Retrieved from https://www.shrm.org/Documents/SHRM-BoCK-FINAL.pdf.

Society for Human Resource Management. (2016b). *Employee satisfaction and engagement: Revitalizing a changing workforce.* Retrieved from https://www.shrm.org/Research/SurveyFindings/Articles/Documents/2016-Employee-Job-Satisfaction-and-Engagement-Report.pdf.

Society for Human Resource Management Foundation. (2016c). *Creating a more human workplace where employees and businesses thrive.* Retrieved from https://www.shrm.org/about/foundation/products/documents/4-16%20human%20workplace-final.pdf.

Van Rooy, D. L., & Oehler, K. (2013). *The evolution of employee opinion surveys: The voice of employees as a strategic management tool.* SHRM-SIOP Science of HR White Paper Series. Retrieved from https://www.shrm.org/Research/Articles/Documents/SIOP%20-%20Employee%20Engagement%20final.pdf.

Wikipedia. (n.d.). *Perceived organizational support.* Retrieved from https://en.wikipedia.org/wiki/Perceived_organizational_support.

Yamada, D. C. (2008). Workplace bullying and ethical leadership. *Journal of Values-Based Leadership, 1*(2). Retrieved from http://papers.ssrn.com/sol3/papers.cfm?abstract_id=1301554

13

Promising Micro Strategies to Minimize Harm to Toxin Handlers

> *Self-care is critical. Eat well, get sleep, exercise and take care of yourself. It's hard to turn it off in my head but taking care of myself is something that I can control and that does help to reduce the stress … but turning it off in my head is hard.*
> *(Daniel, 2018)*

In addition to the organizational, legal, and societal strategies just discussed in Chap. 12, the good news is that there are numerous individual strategies that can be used by practitioners to reduce some of the personal negativity caused by their toxin handling responsibilities. Here are six evidence-based recommendations from some highly experienced HR professionals (Daniel, 2017, 2018, 2019a, b).

Focus on Self-Care

A focus on self-care to help avoid emotional exhaustion and burnout is essential—toxin handlers need to have "a release mechanism" to let go of the negativity and stress.

> *It's important to have a "release valve" so that we don't continue to internalize the feelings and then cause harm to ourselves.*

> *Sometimes there is nothing you can do about it but try to help the person manage it the best they can. So try to find something that makes you laugh—or go to lunch or call a friend.*

Other strategies for self-care include: (1) keeping both physically and emotionally fit; (2) paying close attention to the emotions and behaviors of oneself as well as others; (3) focusing on sources of positive emotions; (4) discussing difficult situations with a trusted confidante; (5) focusing on eating right and getting enough sleep; and (6) finding constructive ways to deal with any remaining emotional stresses (examples suggested were to develop a hobby, participate in a professional networking group, or engage in spiritual practices).

Finding a good coach (particularly one who is also trained as a therapist) and/or contacting the employee assistance program can also be highly useful. In addition, taking yoga and engaging in meditation practices can also help to minimize stress.

Taking time to "unplug" and take "time outs" by scheduling periodic time away from work is also highly recommended, whether through vacations, short weekend trips, or just by taking short breaks during the day. Fundamentally, taking care of oneself is equally as important as taking care of work-related issues. If HR practitioners do not take the time to do this, they will not be able to "stay in the game" for long.

Set Clear Boundaries and Learn to Say "No"

It is critical to set clear boundaries about what you will and will not do. Those boundaries ensure that organizational toxicity is not allowed to permeate the practitioner's life and it also allows them to remain focused on their regular HR duties.

> *I think it's a good thing to have empathy as an HR specialist, for sure, but I think you have to know how to keep good boundaries. Every situation that you encounter [involves] someone didn't get paid right, someone's getting terminated, someone's having conflict with their supervisor. You can get involved and help. But it's one thing to advise and consult, and it's another thing to take on those things and become emotionally involved yourself.*

> *I think you have to set some boundaries. You can't let people monopolize your time. You can't let people just hijack your day with their problems. You can't internalize the negativity. You just have to kind of shake it off because it's not personal.*

> *…you have to know your boundaries—where it cuts off being their issue versus you taking the issue on yourself.*

> *Take a step back and remind yourself that it's not personal. It's not you, it's the situation. Maintain your professionalism and make sure the conversations remain respectful and focused on the issues rather than taking a personal turn.*

You just have to learn to set some boundaries ... You can listen to be empathetic, but you cannot allow that person [the employee] to dominate your time with emotion—negative emotion specifically.

I have a practice that once I leave the office, I don't want to talk about work.

Although hard, there is a need to try to stop feeling guilty about not being able to respond to every employee's request for help. One practitioner put it starkly and candidly like this:

When HR starts being all things to all people, they're nothing to no one.

Develop a Community of Support

Finding or building a community of support so that experiences can be shared with others (particularly fellow HR professionals), either in-house or through external professional networks, can be highly useful. Expanding avenues for increased sharing of experiences may help to diffuse some of the toxicity that would otherwise build up if not released. Local, state, and national SHRM groups can be great places to network and share the joys and frustrations of the job with people who truly understand because they are in the trenches day in and day out. Church or charitable organizations can also be positive places to network and find like-minded people.

Strengthen the Partnership with the Company's EAP and Seek Personal Counseling

Given that most companies have an Employee Assistance Program (EAP) for employees, this may be a place where HR can partner more closely with these counselors and seek their advice about difficult employee situations. Seeking personal counseling early is also recommended to minimize the long-term effects of the role as much as possible.

Pay Close Attention to Work-Life Balance

HR professionals are often passionate and committed to their work, to the employees they serve, as well as to their organizations. They often take on more work than they can handle, causing them to work excessive hours and to experience high levels of stress. As a result, it is important for HR toxin handlers work hard to observe and protect a reasonable work-life balance.

I've tried to watch any overtime that I work so that I do have a balanced life because, although work is important to me, I do have a life outside of the [organization]. It's something that I'm trying to work on right now. But [really observing a health] work-life balance is one of the hardest things for HR professionals [to do].

Learn to resolve what you can and try letting the rest of it stay at work so that it doesn't follow you home at night. But that can be very difficult.

Change Jobs or Leave the Organization Entirely

If the role begins to create so much stress that the toxin handler feels burned out or experiences job-related health issues, there is no shame in calling for a "time out" by moving to a different function within the department—or leaving the organization (and/or the HR profession) entirely.

Dealing with so many negative situations or even toxic or negative people can definitely wear on you, so much that you might decide to leave your organization, or you may even leave the [HR] profession altogether.

So, there you have it … strategies from experienced HR professionals about ways to mitigate the fall-out from dealing with toxic emotions at work. Taking action to implement any or all of these actions will help to reduce the likelihood of stress, exhaustion, compassion fatigue, or burnout, or any of the significant medical issues that can arise when doing this type of work over the long term. Not only will the toxin handler be protected from personal harm, but it also ensures that this valuable work can be continued for the benefit of both employees and the organization.

References

Daniel, T. A. (2017, Winter). Managing toxic emotions at work: An examination of HR's unique role as the "organizational shock absorber". *Employment Relations Today, 43*(4), 13–19.

Daniel, T. A. (2018). *Managing toxic emotions at work: An empirical study of HR's role and its Impact on personal well-being and organizational effectiveness.* https://doi.org/10.13140/RG.2.2.16315.26408.

Daniel, T. A. (2019a, March 13). *Viewpoint: How HR can protect itself from toxic emotions*. Retrieved from https://www.shrm.org/resourcesandtools/hr-topics/employee-relations/pages/viewpoint-how-hr-can-protect-itself-from-toxic-emotions.aspx

Daniel, T. A. (2019b, March 6). *Viewpoint: HR as toxin handlers*. Retrieved from https://www.shrm.org/resourcesandtools/hr-topics/employee-relations/pages/are-you-a-toxin-handler.aspx

14

Can We Reduce Organizational Toxicity by Improving Our Leaders? Hint: Yes, We Can!

There are many ways to finish the sentence "Leadership is …" or "Great leaders are …". In fact, as Stogdill (1974, p. 7) pointed out in a review of leadership research, there are almost as many definitions of leadership as there are authors who write about the topic. This has led Bennis and Nanus (1985) to the cynical observation:

> Never have so many labored so long to say so little. Multiple interpretations of leadership exist, each providing a sliver of insight but each remaining an incomplete and wholly inadequate explanation. (p. 4)

Similarly, in his path-breaking book, *Leadership*, James MacGregor Burns observed that "leadership is one of the most observed and least understood phenomena on earth" (1978, p. 2). To my knowledge, there is still no universal consensus about how leadership should be defined even though scholars and practitioners have been studying the phenomenon for more than a century (Rost, 1991; Northouse, 2013).

Theoretical Perspectives About the Leadership Process

A review of the scholarly studies on leadership shows that there are many different theoretical approaches to explain the complexities of the leadership process (e.g. Bass & Stogdill, 1990; Bryman, 1992; Bryman, Collinson, Grint, Jackson, & Uhl-Bien, 2011; Day & Antonakis, 2012; Gardner, 1990;

Hickman, 2009; Mumford, 2006; Rost, 1991). Some researchers conceptualize leadership as a *trait* (Stogdill, 1948, 1974; Mann, 1959; Lord, DeVader, & Alliger, 1986; Zaccaro, Kemp, & Bader, 2004; Kirkpatrick & Locke, 1991; Bryman, 1992) or as *skills* (Katz, 1955; Mumford, Zaccaro, Harding, Jacobs, & Fleishman, 2000). Others characterize leadership as a *style* or *behavior* (Hemphill & Coons, 1957; Cartwright & Zander, 1960; Katz & Kahn, 1951; Likert, 1961, 1967; Bowers & Seashore, 1966; Blake & McCanse, 1991; Blake & Mouton, 1964, 1985).

Still other researchers view leadership from a *relational standpoint* (e.g. Burns, 1978 and Greenleaf, 1970, among others). These are just a few examples of the voluminous theories used to explain the construct. An, attempt to cover all of the suggested approaches would require writing a book (or several).

Leadership has been studied using both qualitative and quantitative methods in many contexts, including small groups, military groups, and large organizations, among others. Collectively, the research findings on leadership from these areas help to provide a rich picture of this complex process (Northouse, 2013, p. 1). Despite the significant amount of work that has been conducted so far, though, its complexity continues to present "a major challenge to practitioners and researchers interested in understanding the nature of leadership" (Northouse, p. 14).

Use of Power—Personalized Versus Socialized

At its core, leadership is about power and influence which leaders use to get things done. While there are numerous types of power, our interest focuses on the theory espoused by McClelland (1975). He suggests that there are two primary forms of power: *personalized* power—that is, power used for advancing personal gain and influence, and *socialized* power—when the leader's power is used for the benefit of others.

With *personalized* power, the view is selfish and a leader typically achieves short-term results based on self-interest. Common behaviors include: being rude and overbearing, exploitative, dominant, risk, defensive, impulsive, and erratic. It has been theorized that a personalized power orientation might drive toward occupations promoting aggressive strategy and forceful action—like the military (Magee & Langner, 2008). With *socialized* power, the leader's view is primarily focused on others, is longer-term in focus, and empowers others to achieve collective goals. Common behaviors include: collaborative, non-defensive, develops their people, and being a source of strength to both people and the organization which he or she serves.

These two forms of power are not mutually exclusive. A leader can use his power to benefit others but can also gain personally. The real distinction is that when personalized power dominates, the leader gains—most often at the expense of his subordinates and the organization.

Tough/Good Leaders Versus Exceptional Leaders

Given the significant influence that leaders have in an organizational context, it is reasonable to believe that having better leaders will improve the workplace, thereby reducing the organizational toxicity that might otherwise be present. So, what makes a leader exceptional in the eyes of the people that they lead? Based on research initially conducted in a military context (Daniel, 2015, 2017), the characteristics of good leaders and exceptional leaders are discussed below.

What Do Tough/Good Leaders Look Like?

The similarities between good/tough leaders and exceptional leaders are striking. Their behaviors are virtually identically in their use of these core practices which both help to create a positive workplace climate while also achieving strong results:

They *care about their people* (e.g. get to know them on a personal basis, are compassionate, supportive and approachable, and they pay attention to the impact of work on both the soldier and his family).

They *develop their people* (e.g. mentors and coaches regularly, offers honest and constructive feedback, communicate openly and frequently, allow "freedom to maneuver", and provide both family and career counseling).

Moreover, they *exhibit high levels of emotional intelligence* (e.g. they are empathetic, calm under pressure, they establish a climate of mutual trust and respect, they really listen, and they are highly self-aware of their impact on others).

They are intensely *focused on mission accomplishment* (e.g. lead from the front, have high standards for self and others, and exhibit a "tough but fair" approach); and

They *lead with tomorrow in mind* (e.g. make decisions that are in the long-term best interests of the organization).

Their descriptions of good/tough bosses were uniformly consistent in emphasizing their high standards and no-nonsense (but fair) approach:

I think a tough boss has the intention that is in the best interests of the unit. This is what I would expect from any good organization—a high expectation of accomplishing the mission or being the best unit ... I think a tough boss will expect a good outcome but he's not going to destroy his subordinates in the process.

I think the tough leader knows how to turn the hard situation into mentorship or kind of closes the loop and shows you the positive points. Or, even if they're pointing out the negative aspects of it, they're showing it to you in a way to improve you, as opposed to just be screaming and yelling 'I want to know who to blame', 'this is your fault', 'you're a failure'.

My first boss was actually a pretty tough leader, but I felt he was tough but fair so I didn't really ever think he was a toxic leader or a bully. He just had high expectations that were standardized and he expected people to meet them.

Tough leaders work diligently to meet—or exceed—the expectations. It should not be minimized, though—working for a tough boss is clearly challenging. Though the intense focus on results by the tough leader may create tension and stress, subordinates do not take the situations personally, nor do they experience diminished feelings of self-worth or adverse personal or health effects. Instead, they feel a great deal of respect and loyalty to such leaders, viewing them as being "tough but fair" and strongly focused on the long-term best interests of both their subordinates *and* the organization, findings which both support and extend the earlier work of Daniel (2009).

What Makes Exceptional Leaders Different?

Personal Excellence and the Achievement of High Standards

The descriptions of good/tough leaders and exceptional leaders by US Army leaders are virtually identically in their use of these core practices which both help to create a positive workplace climate and achieve results:

They *care about their people* (e.g. get to know them on a personal basis, are compassionate, supportive and approachable, and they pay attention to the impact of work on both the soldier and his family).

They *develop their people* (e.g. mentors and coaches regularly, offers honest and constructive feedback, communicate openly and frequently, allow "freedom to maneuver", and provide both family and career counseling).

Moreover, they *exhibit high levels of emotional intelligence* (e.g. they are empathetic, calm under pressure, they establish a climate of mutual trust and respect, they really listen, and they are highly self-aware of their impact on others).

They are intensely *focused on mission accomplishment* (e.g. lead from the front, have high standards for self and others, and exhibit a "tough but fair" approach); and

They *lead with tomorrow in mind* (e.g. make decisions that are in the long-term best interests of the organization).

Great leaders consistently focus on both personal excellence and the achievement of high standards as evidenced by these observations:

You could tell that he actually cared about people and he didn't just pretend. He would ask personal questions and give you eye contact and listen to the answers and care about the answer. He had a reputation as being extremely competent, but he also had a reputation for really caring about his people—and leaders can't fake that.

They really led from the front. They really embodied everything they said they were going to do. They had a standard and they not only held themselves to that standard, but they also held their subordinates to the same standard.

The best guy I've ever worked for in my life. He's just amazing in every way. He cared about every person [who worked for him]. He worked well and everybody worked together as a team. It was just an amazing experience working for him... He was tough but he kept to his standards.

He was one of those leaders that took you out of your comfort zone, made you strive for excellence. If you tripped, he might give you a little bit of a spanking but it was not "you're terrible and I'm going to end your career"- type, it was "hey you've made a mistake and I'm going to help you improve yourself".

Care and Connect in a Highly Personalized Manner

The crucial differentiator between a *good* leader and a *great* one is that an exceptional leader can be distinguished by the *highly personalized caring* that they extend to both people and their families. The relationships that they establish with people they supervise go well beyond just showing concern. They succeed in creating a positive workplace climate and accomplishing the organization's results by caring and connecting with their people in a deeply personal way (through mentoring, counseling, coaching, and frequent two-way communication). This deep sense of personal commitment and caring creates high levels of mutual trust and makes people feel genuinely valued and respected.

As evidenced by their frequent communication, mentoring, counseling, and efforts to develop the individual for future assignments, exceptional leaders exhibit a holistic personal concern about the people they supervise—not just as people there to do a job, but also as human beings with families, emotions, and real-life concerns and issues. Those who report to an exceptional leader unequivocally know and feel that the leader cares—*really cares*—about them on a personal level.

The significant amount of time invested by an exceptional leader mentoring, counseling, and developing their people results in a high level of mutual trust, inspiration, deep respect, open communication, and unwavering loyalty as these interview comments confirm:

> *I think the level of which they [great leaders] care and the way that they show it is what probably differentiates them most from everyone else. It builds loyalty right off the bat.*

> *He was genuine.*

> *I think they had there was a caring that they gave to us. Maybe [it] was that they cared what was going on in our lives outside of [work]. They were always in touch with us outside of work—making sure that we were doing okay with our families or our friends or what was going on. That really kind of touched us, I think.*

The bottom line: highly effective leaders—whether they are labeled as a great leader or a good/tough boss—are concerned about achieving organizational goals, as well as about their people *and* the long-term best interests of their organization. The crucial difference is that an exceptional leader can be distinguished by the *highly personalized caring* that they extend to both people and their families.

There are many reasons that cause people to quit their jobs. Some of the more common reasons include outdated technologies, lack of necessary resources, manually intensive processes, high benefit costs, conflict-avoidant managers, weak leaders, poor communication or a toxic culture where core values and responsibilities are not clearly defined (Patton, 2020). Improving the quality of the organization's leadership can help not only to reduce turnover and increase profitability, but it can also reduce the unnecessary stress and distraction for employees that are the predictable (and inevitable) by-products of ineffective or toxic leaders (Daniel, 2015, 2018).

Conclusions

Effective leaders know that getting results is critical to the success of their organizations; however, it is those leaders who also excel at caring for and developing their people—for the long-term—who are truly exceptional. It is these extraordinary leaders who help to create organizations where employees can do their best work. They also help to create companies which are profitable and successful, while at the same time reducing the organizational toxicity that causes employees to quit, mentally check out, or suffer from stress-related emotional or medical conditions. That's a win-win in my book—and I would bet that it is in yours too.

References

Bass, B. M., & Stogdill, R. M. (1990). *Handbook of leadership: A survey of theory and research*. New York: Free Press.

Bennis, W., & Nanus, B. (1985). *Leaders: The strategies for taking charge*. New York: Harper & Row.

Blake, R. R., & McCanse, A. A. (1991). *Leadership dilemmas: Grid solutions*. Houston, TX: Gulf Publishing Company.

Blake, R. R., & Mouton, J. S. (1964). *The managerial grid*. Houston, TX: Gulf Publishing Company.

Blake, R. R., & Mouton, J. S. (1985). *The managerial grid III*. Houston, TX: Gulf Publishing Company.

Bowers, D. G., & Seashore, S. E. (1966). Predicting organizational effectiveness with a four-factor theory of leadership. *Administrative Science Quarterly, 11*, 238–263.

Bryman, A. (1992). *Charisma and leadership in organizations*. London: Sage.

Bryman, A., Collinson, D., Grint, K., Jackson, G., & Uhl-Bien, M. (Eds.). (2011). *The SAGE handbook of leadership*. London, UK: Sage.

Burns, J. M. (1978). *Leadership*. New York: Harper & Row.

Cartwright, D., & Zander, A. (1960). *Group dynamics research and theory*. Evanston, IL: Row, Peterson.

Daniel, T. A. (2009). *Tough boss or workplace bully?: A grounded theory study of insights from human resource professionals*. Doctoral Dissertation, Fielding Graduate University. Retrieved from http://gradworks.umi.com/33/50/3350585.html.

Daniel, T. A. (2015). *Crossing the line: An examination of toxic leadership in the U.S. Army*. https://doi.org/10.13140/RG.2.1.2700.4969.

Daniel, T. A. (2017). *An examination of exceptional U.S. Army leaders: What they do and how they impact their employees and organization*. https://doi.org/10.13140/RG.2.2.19317.68326.

Daniel, T. A. (2018). *Managing toxic emotions at work: An empirical study of HR's role and its Impact on personal well-being and organizational effectiveness*. https://doi.org/10.13140/RG.2.2.16315.26408.

Day, D. B., & Antonakis, J. (Eds.). (2012). *The nature of leadership* (2nd ed.). Thousand Oaks, CA: Sage.

Gardner, J. W. (1990). *On leadership*. New York: Free Press.

Greenleaf, R. K. (1970). *The servant as leader*. Westfield, IN: The Greenleaf Center for Servant Leadership.

Hemphill, J. K., & Coons, A. E. (1957). Development of the leader behavior description questionnaire. In R. M. Stogdill & A. E. Coons (Eds.), *Leader behavior: Its description and measurement* (Research Monograph No. 99). Columbus: Ohio State University, Bureau of Business Research.

Hickman, G. R. (Ed.). (2009). *Leading organizations: Perspectives for a new era* (2nd ed.). Thousand Oaks, CA: Sage.

Katz, D., & Kahn, R. L. (1951). Human organization and worker motivation. In L. R. Tripp (Ed.), *Industrial productivity* (pp. 146–171). Madison, WI: Industrial Relations Research Association.

Katz, R. L. (1955). Skills of an effective administrator. *Harvard Business Review, 33*(1), 33–42.

Kirkpatrick, S. A., & Locke, E. A. (1991). Leadership: Do traits matter? *The Executive, 5*, 48–60.

Likert, R. (1961). *New patterns of management*. New York: McGraw-Hill.

Likert, R. (1967). *The human organization: Its management and value*. New York: McGraw-Hill.

Lord, R. G., DeVader, C. L., & Alliger, G. M. (1986). A meta-analysis of the relationship between personality traits and leadership perceptions: An application of validity generalization procedures. *Journal of Applied Psychology, 71*, 402–410.

Magee, J. C., & Langner, C. A. (2008). How personalized and socialized power motivation facilitate antisocial and prosocial decision-making. *Journal of Research in Personality, 42*, 1547–1559.

Mann, R. D. (1959). A review of the relationship between personality and performance in small groups. *Psychological Bulletin, 56*, 241–270.

McClelland, D. C. (1975). *Power: The inner experience*. NY: Irvington.

Mumford, M. D. (2006). *Pathways to outstanding leadership: A comparative analysis of charismatic, ideological, and pragmatic leaders*. Mahway, NJ: Lawrence Erlbaum.

Mumford, M. D., Zaccaro, S. J., Harding, F. D., Jacobs, T. O., & Fleishman, E. A. (2000). Leadership skills for a changing world: Solving complex social problems. *Leadership Quarterly, 11*(1), 11–35.

Northouse, P. G. (2013). *Leadership: Theory and practice* (6th ed.). Thousand Oaks, CA: Sage.

Patton, C. (2020, February 17). What's keeping HR up at night in 2020? *Human Resource Executive*. Retrieved from https://hrexecutive.com/whats-keeping-hr-up-at-night-in-2020/

Rost, J. C. (1991). *Leadership for the twenty-first century*. New York: Praeger.

Stogdill, R. M. (1948). Personal factors associated with leadership: A survey of the literature. *Journal of Psychology, 25*, 35–71.

Stogdill, R. M. (1974). *Handbook of leadership: A survey of theory and research.* New York: Free Press.

Zaccaro, S. J., Kemp, C., & Bader, P. (2004). Leader traits and attributes. In J. Antonakis, A. T. Cianciolo, & R. J. Sternberg (Eds.), *The nature of leadership* (pp. 101–124). Thousand Oaks, CA: Sage.

15

The So-What? Making Sense of It All

It is no longer in doubt that a central aspect of the HR practitioner's role is to act as an organizational toxin handler. HR helps employees deal with toxic emotions created by difficult organizational decisions as well as fears and uncertainty related to difficult situations—like returning to the office during the middle of the COVID-19 pandemic. At the same time, they are also working to keep their organization functioning and profitable by supporting senior leaders.

To do this, they help troubled employees reduce their emotional pain (and the related distraction and reduced productivity that comes with it) so that they can re-focus and get back to work as quickly as possible—clearly, this is a win-win for both impacted employees as well as the organization.

You might remember this conceptual model that was introduced back in Chap. 1 when we started on this journey together. It helps to visually explain the role and undoubtedly makes more sense to you now that you know a whole lot more about this important organizational function:

The heart is key toward visualizing the results of the study given that it demonstrates that HR practitioners are empathetic and compassionate listeners. The arrow to Drives Career Choice demonstrates that their empathetic and compassionate nature drives their career choice—becoming an HR professional. The arrow back to the heart demonstrates that it is this combination of empathy and compassion that drives employees to seek their counsel (and also because of the nature of the HR role itself).

The original version of this chapter was revised to add the missing figure 15.1 in chapter 15. The correction to this chapter is available at https://doi.org/10.1007/978-3-030-51685-7_17.

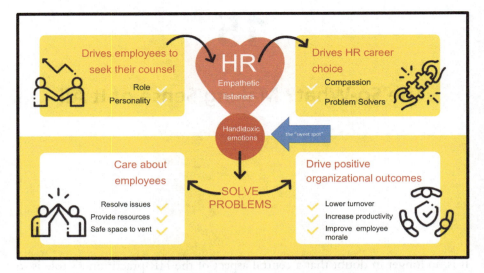

Fig. 15.1 Conceptual model of HR's role as organizational toxin handler (Daniel, 2018)

The "sweet spot" is when they solve problems for both employees and the organization by being "HR fixers". They do this by providing care and concern for employees so that they feel understood and valued, while maintaining a sharp awareness of the need to keep their organizations functioning and profitable. Managing this dual role is a delicate and complex balancing act that creates a great deal of stress for HR practitioners.

- *For Employees*:

- HR practitioners show that they care and help to solve problems for employees by empathetic listening, suggesting solutions and providing resources, by working behind the scenes and providing a safe space, through confidential counseling, by strategizing communications and reframing difficult messages, and by consulting, facilitating, and coaching/advising managers.

- *For the Organization*:

- HR's work as a toxin handler helps to drive positive organizational outcomes by lowering turnover, increasing productivity, and improving employee morale.

Although the role of a toxin handler is important to organizations, when HR practitioners do this work, the work is mostly invisible to senior leaders due to the expectation that HR will maintain confidentiality and privacy for employees who seek their help. As a result, they do not feel that the work is recognized or appreciated. Over time, engaging in this helping role tends to negatively affect their well-being through increased levels of stress, burnout, emotional and physical exhaustion, and an increased intent to quit.

While HR is often "front and center" in responding to employees in need, it is important to note that HR cannot (and should not be expected to) do it alone. Senior leaders must take an active and visible role in efforts to reduce organizational toxicity. If they fail to do this, employees can easily misinterpret their absence to suggest that they do not find the issue to be serious enough to warrant their time and attention or, worse yet, that they simply don't care.

It is clear that numerous workplace situations, including layoffs, harassment, discrimination, mergers and acquisitions, personality conflicts, or an abusive boss can generate intense emotional pain for employees—feelings like anger, frustration, stress, disappointment, and even fear. Although these types of events are somewhat inevitable, it is the way organizations handle them—or do not—that can create a serious problem for both employees and, ultimately, the organizations that they serve.

Painful emotions and high stress are unfortunate by-products of these commonplace situations—a true occupational hazard. Ignoring these reactions puts the organization at risk; conversely, responding to and helping employees deal with those problems puts the toxin handler at risk, making it a dangerous and mostly thankless job (Daniel, 2018):

I think that we play a critical role in keeping all the balls in the air. I say that a lot. It's the fact that we are able to diffuse so many volatile situations or the fact that we're able to reason with people that are otherwise not listening or not hearing what's being said or understanding what has to be done to get the work done. ***I think we have a huge impact on the organizational effectiveness, and I think nobody's ever going to see that until it's not being done.*** *I do think it's a very key piece in this and I don't think that people really understand it. It's a thankless job.*

Despite the risks, however, toxin handlers in HR step up to provide this compassionate care to employees in pain because they know the work is essential to their efforts to create and sustain a humane and respectful workplace culture. However, they face a *precarious balancing act* between the competing role demands of helping employees while at the same time supporting (and often challenging) senior leaders and protecting the interests of their company. The HR role is complex and paradoxical in nature which only serves to exacerbate the stress experienced by HR practitioners at work. As a result, they often pay a high price for doing the work in terms of the negative impact to their own personal well-being.

Creating and sustaining a psychologically healthy workplace—one that is devoid of frequent toxicity—benefit both employees *and* their organizations. The empirical evidence unequivocally confirms what we all already know intuitively—a respectful workplace environment results in higher levels of employee morale and job satisfaction, lower turnover, reduced health costs, higher productivity, and greater profitability for the organization. Coincidentally, demonstrating the courage and leadership necessary to reduce organizational toxicity—and to proactively address the fallout of toxic emotions when it exists—is also likely to result in a more effective and admired HR department.

This comment from an HR practitioner probably best sums up the impact of the organizational toxin handling role on people (Daniel, 2018):

> *I feel like the role of the HR professional is to take what is most likely going to be one of the worst days of this person's life and make it as bearable as possible.*

Working as an HR practitioner inside an organization is hard, and some days it can be *very* hard. HR practitioners know that helping employees deal with the pain caused by toxic emotions caused by difficult workplace decisions or situations is not only the right thing to do, but that it is also good for business. For this work to be sustainable, though, organizations will need to make these responsibilities explicit in the relevant HR job descriptions, and take affirmative steps to recognize, support, and reward organizational toxin handlers—who are, for both employees and their organizations, truly often-invisible heroes.

I am proud to be an organizational toxin handler and grateful to be part of this noble profession—and I hope that you are too. HR hero—that has a nice ring to it, doesn't it? And as they say, if the cape fits, I hope you will wear it proudly. You've no doubt earned it.

Reference

Daniel, T. A. (2018). *Managing toxic emotions at work: An empirical study of HR's role and its Impact on personal well-being and organizational effectiveness.* https://doi.org/10.13140/RG.2.2.16315.26408.

16

Epilogue: A Manifesto for a New (and Better) Future

The emotional dimensions of HR's organizational role have been discussed at great length in this book. Numerous strategies to minimize the impact of our compassionate natures on our own personal well-being while still being able to do the work we love have also been identified.

It is very seductive to be "busy" as HR professionals—busy about our "to do" lists, busy answering emails and phone calls, and busy helping employees deal with stressful emotions and problems that often take over our workdays, leaving the bulk of our "real work" to be completed after hours. All of this "busyness" causes an additional layer of stress that piles onto our already stressful workdays which are filled with managing conflict, resolving problems, and helping employees to deal with the organizational toxicity that is inevitable in a world that runs 24/7.

I want to close this book with a personal challenge to each of you, dear readers, to think—and really think hard—about some important questions. Your answers will impact how you choose to operate both at work and at home, and they will, hopefully, help guide you into a future that may even be more satisfying than you ever thought possible. Here goes:

What does it mean to live a good life? What about a productive life? How about a happy life? And perhaps the most important question of all: how can we best use our 80 years on earth (if we are really, really lucky) to live out the answer to these important questions?

Consider what really matters to you—your core values—those sacrosanct ideals by which you live and that drive how you spend much of your time. Is it work, money, family, faith, fame, or some combination of these important things?

Now, think about how you actually spend your days. If you are like most practitioners, your time is often spent doing things that you really don't want to do or that you really don't think are all that important. If this is the case in your work life or at home (or worse yet, both), you may be pursuing someone else's idea of success or just operating in default mode. Either way, it may be worth thinking more critically about how you really want to spend your precious 29,220 days on this planet.

One of the most important conversations that we can have—with our children and with ourselves—is to discuss what we actually mean by success. Why? Because how we define success determines a great deal about how we will spend our time (and whom we will spend much of it with). Is a successful life defined by being a decent, thoughtful, and kind human being and finding ways to enjoy the "normal" (but not particularly noteworthy) days that tend to dominate most of our existence? Or is a successful life defined by the money, cars, jewelry, and houses that one accumulates along the way?

I would venture to say that when most of us look back at the good times of our life—those times when we felt truly content and fulfilled—it will be the regular days when everything was at least "just okay" that we are likely to miss the most. To me, life's true blessings are unexpected visits or calls from one of our sons, our boys, reading a good book on a weekend afternoon, or watching a sunset with my husband. Sadly, though, these days are sometimes invisible to us because they are so "normal"—and we end up missing them as a result.

Why? Because we are all too often distracted by our need to prove the legitimacy of our existence by being "busy" all of the time, or by our quest for money and power (and some add fame to the mix as well). A focus on those outcomes is society's current definitions of success—but is it yours?

The problem with this definition is, though, that an all-consuming focus on the accumulation of money and power creates a life that is difficult to manage and maintain, and too often devoid of joy and connection. It is difficult for anyone to sustain the expected workload or the long hours required to "make it" for any extended period of time. Time is in short supply for all of us. There are only 24 hours in anyone's day, no matter how productive you are or how little you sleep. The end result is that something usually goes wrong.

Arianna Huffington accurately summed up the current situation during her commencement address to the graduating class of Smith College in 2013 (Huffington, 2013):

16 Epilogue: A Manifesto for a New (and Better) Future

Don't buy society's definition of success, because it's not working for anyone. It's not working for women. It's not working for men. It's not working for polar bears, and it's not working for the cicadas that are apparently about to emerge and swarm us. It's only truly working for those who make pharmaceuticals for stress, diabetes, heart disease, sleeplessness, and high blood pressure.

Is it just me, or does there seem to be a disconnect between our espoused values and those we actually live by? While we often claim to value service, kindness, and compassion to others, what we actually reward and celebrate are "winners"—even if their "win" is based on unprofessional, unethical, or even abusive conduct.

What if we reimagine success and incorporate a more holistic approach that includes consideration of how each of us stack up in several other important realms as well? Perhaps a three-part conceptual framework could be a start to help us each assess where we are and how we are doing:

- *Regard for Self*: What is the condition of our personal well-being? Do we engage in healthy behaviors (eat healthfully, exercise regularly, engage in reflection, refrain from smoking, and make sleep a priority)? Do we continually engage in learning and other forms of self-improvement? Do we maintain a strong social network so that we stay connected with others?
- *Regard for Others*: Do we listen and show empathy for problems experienced by friends, family, and colleagues? and
- *Regard for Society*: Do we stay informed about important issues so that we can make good decisions? Do we offer our time, talent, and resources to those in need? Do we show up when it is time to vote?

Journalist Courtney Martin (2016) eloquently captured the situation in a beautiful TED Talk several years ago where she told the audience:

Turns out, the biggest danger is not failing to achieve the American Dream. The biggest danger is achieving a dream that you don't actually believe in. So, don't do that. Do the harder, more interesting thing, which is to compose a life where what you do every single day, the people you give your best love and ingenuity and energy to, aligns as closely as possible with what you believe. That, not something as mundane as making money, is a tribute to your ancestors. **That is the beautiful struggle.**

To design and live the lives that we want—and not just the ones we settle for—requires us to redefine and reimagine what it really means to be successful. As practitioners, we are among the lucky ones. We have already entered a profession that, by its nature, gives us many opportunities to operate more in sync with our personal values and to feel that we have made a positive difference in people's lives. By helping employees manage high-stress situations, HR enables other employees to stay focused and do their jobs. Without them, the organizational toxicity would continue to build, resulting in higher and higher levels of turnover, increased health costs, more litigation, and reduced levels of employee morale, productivity, and profitability.

As this book highlights, even though HR, OD, and coaching professionals experience a great deal of satisfaction from helping people, the work is stressful and often comes at a cost to our personal health and well-being. In an effort to mitigate some of the inherent tension caused by our organizational role, what if we challenge ourselves to drop our persistent need to be "busy" and, instead, consciously focus on doing *more* of what matters to us and to our organizations, and *less* on the things that don't?

Perhaps most importantly, though, what if we accept the challenge to care for ourselves with the same level of energy that we expend to care for others? It is not weak, selfish, or self-indulgent to acknowledge our limitations and take a time out to engage in self-care practices. In fact, it actually increases our capacity to help others. Although it may seem obvious, it bears repeating here: it helps no one for us to "crash and burn" or, worse yet, leave the profession altogether.

Most definitely, caring for others and fixing problems is a big part of what we do—and by most reports, we are quite good at it. However, placing more emphasis on also caring for our own personal well-being will allow us to maintain our energy reserves and keep our motivation levels high so that we can continue to positively impact the lives of those with whom we live and work *and* the organizations that we serve. That sure sounds like success to me. What about you?

References

Huffington, A. (2013). *Smith College 2013 Commencement Speech* [Online]. Retrieved from https://www.smith.edu/about-smith/smith-history/commencement-speakers/college-events-commencement-speech-2013.

Martin, C. (2016). *The new American dream.* TED Talk [Online]. Retrieved from https://www.ted.com/talks/courtney_e_martin_the_new_american_dream?language=en

Correction to: The So-What? Making Sense of It All

Correction to:

Chapter 15 in: Teresa A. Daniel, *Organizational Toxin Handlers*, https://doi.org/10.1007/978-3-030-51685-7_15

The original version of the book was inadvertently published without adding the figure in chapter 15. The chapter has now been updated with the missing figure.

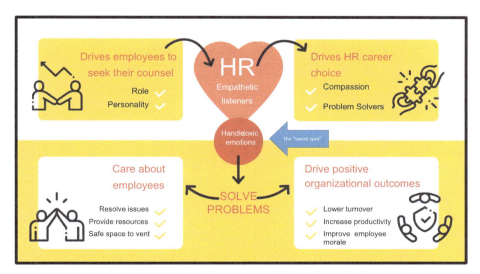

Fig. 15.1 Conceptual model of HR's role as organizational toxin handler (Daniel, 2018)

The updated version of the chapter can be found at
https://doi.org/10.1007/978-3-030-51685-7_15

© The Author(s) 2020
T. A. Daniel, *Organizational Toxin Handlers*, https://doi.org/10.1007/978-3-030-51685-7_17

Appendix A: Executive Summary of the Research Study

Title of the Study—*Managing Toxic Emotions at Work: An Empirical Study of HR's Role and Its Impact on Personal Well-Being and Organizational Effectiveness* (2018)

Author—Teresa A. Daniel, JD, PhD (Principal Investigator) with Chris Gray (Research Assistant), Sullivan University, Louisville, KY.

Purpose—Toxin handlers are people within an organization who "voluntarily shoulder the sadness, frustration, bitterness, and the anger that are endemic to organizational life"—collectively referred to as toxic emotions (Frost, 2003, 2004, 2006). This study was designed to explore the perceptions of HR professionals about their role in handling toxic emotions at work and to examine the impact of that work on both their personal well-being and the effectiveness of their organizations. A secondary aim was to explore how organizations can minimize the need for toxin handling and reduce the harm caused to those who do this important work.

Design/Methodology/Approach—This empirical, qualitative study consisted of a series of in-depth, semi-structured interviews with 26 highly educated and experienced HR professionals. The analysis, interpretations, and conclusions about the data were conducted in accord with the constructivist, grounded theory methodology, using constant comparative analysis.

Findings—The study found that 58% of the participants helped employees deal with toxic emotions on a daily basis. Participants were unanimous in their view that toxin handling work was disproportionately assumed by HR practitioners, and three-quarters of the participants (73.1%) felt that this work was not recognized or appreciated by senior leaders in their organizations, largely due to the expectation that HR will maintain confidentiality and privacy for employees who seek their help.

When helping employees and their organizations deal with toxic emotions at work, HR practitioners engage in six core activities: empathetic listening, suggest solutions and provide resources, work behind the scenes and provide a safe space, confidential counseling, strategize communications and reframe difficult messages, and coach and advise managers. They take on the toxin handling role due to their empathetic and compassionate natures, as well as their strong ability to solve problems. In addition, some participants observed that it was an inherent part of the HR role itself (even though these duties were not typically included in their official job description).

By helping employees manage high-stress situations at work, HR toxin handlers enable other employees to stay focused and do their jobs. Without them, the organizational toxicity would continue to build, resulting in higher levels of turnover, increased health costs, more litigation, and reduced levels of employee morale and productivity. However, the toxin handling role is dangerous because of the personal risk it poses to the HR practitioner's well-being over time. Participants reported significant physical and emotional exhaustion, feelings of sadness and anger, high stress, lack of sleep, and burnout. In addition, their personal relationships, overall health, and home life were also negatively affected. This caused some of the study's participants to seek personal counseling as a result of the excessive strain.

The study resulted in the development of a new grounded theory and conceptual model which suggested that a central aspect of the HR practitioner's role is to act as an organizational toxin handler. In addition, practical recommendations were identified—both individual and systemic—which may help to minimize the harm to HR practitioners while ensuring that this important work can continue to contribute to positive organizational outcomes.

Limitations of the Study—This was an exploratory study. We can only indicate that our findings are suggestive and representative of a small—but important—group of highly experienced and highly educated HR professionals who participated in this study. As a result, we advise caution when attempting to generalize these findings to any other group. Other potential limitations were also noted.

Suggestions for Future Research—Future studies to examine the linkages between emotional intelligence and empathy with toxin handling would be of use. In addition, studies to explore whether expanded training or more organizational communication may help to reduce levels of toxic emotions at work would also be of interest. Other potential recommendations for future research were also noted.

Originality/Value/Implications—The study resulted in the development of a new grounded theory and conceptual model which suggested that a central aspect of the HR practitioner's role is to act as an organizational toxin handler. This study also confirmed the five core actions of a toxin handler first identified in Frost's (2003, 2004, 2006) ground-breaking work. Further, this empirical study, one of the earliest of its kind to focus on the HR profession, extended Frost's earlier work by finding that coaching and advising managers was an additional core action for toxin handlers working in the HR domain. Finally, the study yielded practical recommendations—both individual and systemic—that may help to minimize the negative impact of toxin handling on HR practitioners while ensuring that this important work can continue to contribute to positive organizational outcomes.

Keywords—Toxic emotions, Toxin handler, Human Resources, HR professional, Well-being, Organizational effectiveness, Organizational toxicity, Constructivist grounded theory

Appendix B: Technical Report

Managing Toxic Emotions at Work:
An Empirical Study of HR's Role and Its Impact on Personal Well-Being and Organizational Effectiveness
Principal Investigator
Teresa A. Daniel, JD, PhD
Dean and Professor—Human Resource Leadership Program Sullivan University
Louisville, KY 40205
tdaniel@sullivan.edu
606-922-3384
Doctoral Research Assistant
Chris Gray
Sullivan University IRB Reference Number: IRB #01102018-02
© Copyright by Teresa A. Daniel, JD, PhD, October 2018. All rights reserved.

Overview of the Study

Systematic Review of the Literature

The first phase of the project consisted of a systematic review of what is broadly known about what toxin handlers actually do, why they do it, their impact on organizational effectiveness, and what their organization can do to alleviate the negative impact of this important role on those who elect to do it. The result of this initial work was published in the practitioner-focused *Employment Relations Today* journal and is incorporated herein by reference. See: Daniel, T. A. (2017, Winter). Managing toxic emotions at work: An examination of HR's unique role as the "organizational shock absorber". *Employment Relations Today, 43*(4), 13–19.

Funding, IRB Approval, and the Secondary Literature Review

Request for Funding

This research study was conceptualized, designed, and submitted to the Sullivan University Faculty Research Grant program with a request for funding consideration during the fall of 2017 call for proposals. On December 15, 2017, a grant in the amount of $5,000.00 was awarded to conduct the study.

IRB Approval

An application was then submitted to the Institutional Review Board of Sullivan University requesting permission to proceed with the study. The study was officially approved by the IRB on April 19, 2018.

Secondary Literature Review

A secondary review of the relevant literature was conducted to ensure that all contemporary studies had been incorporated into this study. A vast body of literature about the broader concept of emotional labor was identified (e.g. *see*, O'Brien & Linehan, 2014, 2016; Devi, 2016; Wargnier, 2014; Hochschild, 1983, among many others). While it was found to be a very closely related area of study, it was determined that a more complete examination of this topic, how it is similar or different from toxin handling, and its specific impact on HR professionals should be included as a suggestion for future research.

Some additional literature which discussed the concepts of saturation and the appropriate sample size for a grounded theory study was identified and has been included in the Evaluation of the Study section which appears later in this report.

Data Collection and Analysis

Research Questions

Specifically, the goal of this study was to provide answers to these specific questions:

1. What is the role of HR in handling issues of intense and highly charged emotions at work?
2. Why do HR practitioners take on the role of toxin handler within their organizations?
3. What impact does the role of toxin handler have on HR practitioners, both personally and professionally?
4. How does the work of a toxin handler impact organizational effectiveness?
5. What strategies can toxin handlers pursue in order to reduce the negative impact of this role?
6. What strategies can organizations pursue in order to minimize the harm to toxin handlers?

Overview of the Method

The design for this study involved a qualitative strategy of inquiry using constructivist, grounded theory as the method (Charmaz, 2006, 2014). The constructivist ontological foundation for theory building "places priority on the studied phenomenon and sees both data and analysis as created from shared experiences and relationships with participants and other sources of data" (Charmaz, 2014, p. 239).

According to Charmaz (2006, 2014), the foundational and key components of a well-designed grounded theory study include:

- Simultaneous involvement in data collection and analysis
- Constructing analytic codes and categories from data, not from preconceived logically deduced hypotheses
- Using the constant comparison method, which involves making comparisons during each stage of the analysis
- Advancing theory development during each step of data collection and analysis

- Memo-writing to elaborate categories, specify their properties, define relationships between categories and identify gaps
- Sampling aimed toward theory construction, not for population representativeness
- Conducting the literature review after developing an independent analysis

Rationale for Method Selection

Lee, Mitchell, and Sabylnski (1999) describe four purposes for qualitative research that have implications for the study of HR leadership: theory generation, theory elaboration, theory testing, and critical theory development. Moreover, the use of a qualitative approach and, specifically, the selection of grounded theory as a methodology, is widely advocated for social science research (e.g. Van Maanen, 1983; Parry, 1998; Conger, 1998; Bryman, 2004; Conger & Toegel, 2002).

In particular, the method allows for theory that is inductively derived and emerges from, and is grounded in, the experiences of those living the phenomenon of interest. What this means is that the theory is discovered, developed, and provisionally verified through systematic data collection and analysis of data pertaining to that phenomenon. Therefore, data collection, analysis, and theory development stand in reciprocal relationship with each other (Charmaz, 2006. 2014).

Conger and Toegel (2002) provide further support for the selection of this approach. They stress that qualitative methods are an important tool for the study of organizations and leadership for three key reasons: (1) this tool can help us understand how leadership is differentially exercised at various organizational levels; (2) given that leadership is a dynamic process, qualitative research methods can add depth and richness that is lacking in data gleaned from questionnaires; and (3) because leadership is considered by some researchers and theories to be a socially constructed role, qualitative methods can aid in understanding the construct from multiple perspectives.

Moreover, grounded theory "helps researchers understand complex social processes", and is particularly appropriate when exploring relatively new concepts in more depth (Suddaby, 2006; Conger, 1998). In fact, key paradigm shifts in the study of organizations and leadership have come from qualitative studies (e.g. Conger & Toegel, 2002; citing Bennis & Nanus, 1985 and Mintzberg, 1973).

Grounded theory provides a detailed, rigorous, and systematic method of analysis, which has the advantage of reserving the need for the researcher to conceive preliminary hypotheses. As a result, it provides greater freedom to explore the research area and allow issues to emerge (Bryant, 2002), making it particularly useful in providing rigorous insight into areas that are relatively unknown by the researcher.

Charmaz (2014, p. 233) explains the importance of theorizing in a grounded theory study as follows:

> Theories flash illuminating insights and make sense of murky musings and knotty problems. The ideas fit. Phenomena and relationships between them you only sensed beforehand become visible. Still, theories can do more. A theory can alter your viewpoint and change your consciousness. Through it, you can see the world from a different vantage point and create new meanings of it. Theories have an internal logic and more or less coalesce into coherent forms.

Charmaz also suggests that theorizing "entails the practical activity of engaging the world and of constructing abstract understanding about and within it" (Charmaz, 2006, p. 128). As a result, the fundamental contribution of grounded theory methods resides in the fact that it can infuse a study with the tools to "bring meanings into view" (Charmaz, 2006, p. 129), which was a key intent of our study.

Finally, as noted by Lee (1999), while qualitative research "is not well suited for issues of prevalence, generalizability, and calibration", it is highly useful for purposes such as theory generation or elaboration. As a result, this approach was determined to be the most appropriate one for this empirical study.

Data Collection

Sample Selection

The selection process relied on non-probability, purposive sampling and targeted a specific population believed to possess unique knowledge about the topic of toxin handling within organizations (Creswell, 1998, 2013). Specifically, to be included in the study, the participants were required to meet these criteria:

(1) Be an *active* Human Resource professional; and
(2) Have at least five (5) years of relevant experience

The rationale for restricting participation to HR practitioners who met these criteria was founded on the belief that individuals with at least five years of service would have had more opportunities to observe and experience toxin handling responsibilities in person. It is believed that this experience provided for a more robust and well-rounded perspective of the issue. The study was also restricted to only currently *active* HR personnel. As a result, we intended to provide a contemporary examination of the issue as it currently exists within organizations at this point in time.

Recruitment Strategy

Recruitment of participants for the study took place during a three-month period, beginning in May and closing at the end of July 2018. An open invitation to participate in the research was included in the May 2018 issue of the Kentucky Society for Human Resource Management organization's monthly magazine. In addition, an invitation to participate was extended via email to members of the Sullivan University Human Resource Leadership Program Advisory Board, to human resource employees employed by the U.S. Department of Veteran's Affairs, as well to academic and practitioner colleagues of both the principal investigator and doctoral research assistant (via email, word of mouth, and through a post to the principal investigator's connections on LinkedIn, the professional networking site). All recruitment efforts conformed to the criteria pre-approved by the Sullivan University Institutional Review Board.

Semi-Structured Interviews

Semi-structured, in-depth interviews with 26 individuals who met the study's sample criteria were conducted either in person, via Skype or Collaborate, and/or by telephone. Each interview lasted 45 minutes to one hour. The interviews were digitally recorded after both informed consent and demographic information was obtained from each participant. Each interview was transcribed verbatim by a professional transcriptionist who signed a confidentiality agreement before commencing any of the work.

Interviews were continued until the researcher identified clear signals of data saturation which included repetition of information and the confirmation of emerging conceptual categories (Aldiabat & Le Navenec, 2018; Suddaby, 2006; Thomson, 2004, 2011). We determined that saturation had been reached at the conclusion of 12 interviews; however, we continued to collect data until 26 interviews were completed in an effort to ensure that "(a) no new or relevant data seem to emerge regarding a category, (b) the category is well developed in terms of its properties and dimensions demonstrating variation, and (c) the relationships among categories are well-established and validated" (Thomson, 2011).

After these additional interviews were conducted and the data was re-evaluated, we concluded that the data collection phase of our study was, indeed, complete and that absolutely no new information was forthcoming (Bonde, 2013; Thomson, 2011; Suddaby, 2006).

Demographic Profile of the Participants

Twenty-six HR practitioners were interviewed for this study, of which 76.9% were female and 84.6% were Caucasian. The majority of participants fell into the 36–49 year age range (46.15%) while 30.8% were 50 years or older. The participants were overwhelmingly married (76.9%). Of note, 61.5% of the participants had earned a master's degree and half (50.0%) of the participants had 20 or more years of HR-related experience, so it was both a highly educated and highly experienced participant group. Over half of the participants identified their role as "HR generalist" (57.9%), while 15.4% were currently in the role of HR director. Table B1.1 contains more specific and complete demographic data of the study's respondents.

Analysis of the Data

The analysis, interpretations, and conclusions about the data were conducted in accordance with the constructivist, grounded theory methodology outlined by Charmaz (2006, 2014), using constant comparative analysis. The resulting theory is an interpretation given that it is, in part, dependent on the researcher's view of the data (Charmaz, 2014). Using this approach gave priority to showing "patterns and connections rather than to linear reasoning" and did not attempt to determine causality (Charmaz, 2006, p. 126).

Throughout the process, the central goal was to look for similar patterns of description. The investigators read through all of the interview transcripts numerous times to ensure accuracy and then each independently coded the data by hand (Lincoln & Guba, 1985). Each new description was

Table B1.1 Demographic data of study respondents

Demographics	Total n	% of participants (n = 26)
Gender		
Male	6	23.1
Female	20	76.9
Race		
Black or African American	2	7.7
Asian	1	3.8
Caucasian	22	84.6
Two or More Races	1	3.8
Age		
26–35 years	2	7.7
36–49 years	12	46.2
50–59 years	8	30.8
60–69 years	4	15.4
Marital status		
Single	2	7.7
Married	20	76.9
Divorced	4	15.4
Education level		
Some College	1	3.8
Bachelor's Degree	8	30.8
Master's Degree	16	61.5
Doctoral Degree	1	3.8
Years of experience		
5–9 years	4	15.4
10–19 years	9	34.6
20 or more years	13	50.0
Position title		
HR Generalist	15	57.7
HR Officer	2	7.7
HR Manager	2	7.7
HR Director	4	15.4
HR Supervisor	1	3.8
HR Professor	1	3.8
HR Consultant	1	3.8
Organizational sector		
Government	16	61.5
Civilian	10	38.5

systematically compared to decide whether it fit into an existing category or represented a new one.

The data collection resulted in 26 hours of taped interview transcripts which were transcribed into written form for analysis purposes as well. The primary investigator and doctoral student met and exchanged written documents and notes on several occasions to discuss their independent coding of the interview transcripts and the emerging categories. The data was coded both by hand and also by using DeDoose, a software program designed to assist in the analysis of qualitative data. Ultimately, the codes and categories that emerged were reviewed and compared by both investigators and the coding process was guided by the research questions. The comparison of the codes and categories resulted in nuanced and very minor disagreement which was resolved through on-going discussions until consensus was reached about all codes and categories.

During the initial cycle of open coding, we named segments of data with a label that simultaneously categorized, summarized, and accounted for each piece of data. Our ultimate aim was to remain open to analytic possibilities and to make "an interpretative rendering that … illuminates studied life" (Charmaz, 2014, p. 111). This provided us freedom and openness to creatively look for new ideas and patterns emerging from the data instead of relying on earlier concepts suggested by other researchers (Charmaz, 2006, pp. 47–48). This phase of the analysis also allowed us to generate preliminary categories.

For the second cycle of focused coding, codes that described similar behaviors were grouped into more general and abstract units of analysis which helped to advance the theoretical direction of our work. This stage of coding had the effect of reducing the large number of initial codes and allowed us to further abstract the categories and begin to link them. Theoretical sampling was used to seek and collect pertinent data to elaborate and refine categories of our emerging theory (Charmaz, 2014, p. 192).

Analytic memo writing was used to record our observations as we analyzed the data. We also diagrammed potential relationships between concepts. These memos and diagrams helped to "catch our thoughts, capture comparisons and connections, and crystallize questions and directions" to pursue. They also helped us to "make discoveries about our data, emerging categories, the developing frame of our analysis—and perhaps about [ourselves]" (Charmaz, 2014, p. 162). This method of recording research notes—both conceptually and visually—allowed us to link the raw data with theoretical thinking and also assisted in the overall data analysis and reporting. Memo writing helped to force connections among concepts and resulted in the discovery of patterns, thereby helping to generate a more complex theory, rather than just a simple description of the data.

A second review of the existing literature was conducted as a part of the memo sorting process (Charmaz, 2014, p. 307). This helped to ensure which literature was relevant and if any additional literature should be included in the study. We answered that question in the negative with respect to the topic of toxic emotion handling, but we did incorporate some new literature which confirmed the adequacy of our sample size and identified the related topic of emotional labor and HR as a closely related area that is ripe for future study.

Through this iterative process, there was a cyclic interplay between data collection, analysis, and theory building (Parry, 1998). Further abstraction and interpretive rendering resulted in the emergence of a theory and conceptual model.

Evaluation of the Study Criteria for Evaluating Grounded Theory Research

Charmaz (2014) outlined a set of criteria for evaluating grounded theory studies which include: credibility, originality, resonance, and usefulness (pp. 337–338). In terms of originality, this is one of the first empirical studies of its kind to examine the specific role of HR professionals in handling toxic emotions at work and the impact of this work on organizational effectiveness. The sample consisted of 26 highly educated HR practitioners, each with significant field experience, which added to the study's credibility. In combination, these factors increased the resonance, usefulness, and subsequent value of our contribution to both HR practitioners and scholars.

Appropriateness of the Sample Size

Hennink, Kaiser, and Marconi (2016) opined that *code saturation* (where researchers have "heard it all") can be reached at nine interviews while *meaning saturation* (when researchers "understand it all") can be reached between 16–24 interviews. Meeting both types of saturation, using both objective and objective data, is believed to afford the best guarantee of study rigor (Morse, 2015a).

We reached both "code saturation" and "meaning saturation" and ended the study having completed 26 interviews of study participants. Theoretical saturation is defined as "the phase of qualitative data analysis in which the researcher has continued sampling and analyzing data until no new data appear and all concepts of the theory are well-developed … and their linkages to other concepts are clearly described" (Morse, 2004, p. 1123). We also reached theoretical saturation, the point at which it is appropriate to cease data collection.

The sample size in this current study exceeded the 12 interviews deemed necessary for saturation as suggested by Guest, Bunce, and Johnson (2006) and fell between the range of 10 to 30 interviews deemed necessary for saturation as demonstrated by a review of 100 grounded theory studies conducted by Thomson (2011). Our sample also met the suggested criteria of between 12 and 60 recommended by Adler and Adler (2012) and also fell between 20 and 50 suggested by Ragin (2012). Moreover, the sample size also exceeded 15 interviews which Bertaux (1981, p. 35) opined to be the smallest acceptable sample for any qualitative research study. In support of these sample ranges, Charmaz (2006, p. 114) also confirmed that "a small study with 'modest claims' might achieve saturation quicker than a study that is aiming to describe a process that spans disciplines."

To achieve rigor and saturation, Morse (2015b) recommended that researchers use the following strategies: "prolonged engagement, persistent observation, and thick, rich description; inter-rater-reliability, negative case analysis; peer review or debriefing; clarifying researcher bias; member checking; external audits, and triangulation" (p. 1212). With the exception of member checking and an external audit, these strategies were utilized in this study to further ensure both rigor and data saturation.

Ritchie, Lewis, and Elam (2003) identified seven factors that might also affect the potential size (and adequacy) of a qualitative study sample: "the heterogeneity of the population; the number of selection criteria; the extent to which 'nesting' of criteria is needed; groups of special interest that require intensive study; multiple samples within one study; types of data collection methods used; and the budget and resources available".

Jette, Grover, and Keck (2003) suggested that expertise in the chosen topic can reduce the number of participants needed in a study as well. Green and Thorogood (2009, p. 120) have stated that "the experience of *most* qualitative researchers (emphasis added) is that in interview studies, little that is 'new' comes out of transcripts after you have interviewed 20 or so people".

Similarly, Bonde (2013) determined five factors that influence the researcher's decision to stop further data collection and make a determination that saturation has been reached: (1) the scope and complexity of the phenomena under study and the method of data collection; (2) the homogeneity of the sample and experience of participants in the research topic; (3) expertise of the qualitative researcher; (4) available resources (e.g. budget, time, availability of participants); and (5) the influence of the intended audience on sample size and data saturation (e.g. qualitative researchers often increase their sample size to convince their quantitative colleagues who are typically more familiar with large samples).

Guest et al. (2006) carried out a systematic analysis of their own data from a study of 60 women involving reproductive health care in Africa. They examined the codes developed from their 60 interviews in an attempt to assess the point at which their data returned no new codes (and had therefore reached saturation). Their findings suggested that data saturation had occurred at a very early stage. Of the 36 codes developed during their study, 34 were developed from their first 6 interviews, and 35 were developed after only 12 interviews. Their conclusion was that, for studies with a high level of homogeneity among the population, "a sample of six interviews may [be] sufficient to enable development of meaningful themes and useful interpretations" (p. 78).

It should be noted also that this sample size met the range of 20–30 interviews for a grounded theory study recommended by Creswell (1998, 2013), the target of 25 participants suggested by Charmaz (2006, p. 114) and Dworkin (2012), the range of 30–50 advised by Morse (1994, p. 225), and the average sample size of 25 interviews outlined by Thomson (2011). While these ranges are offered as guidance to researchers, it should also be noted that "the authors do not tend to present empirical arguments as to why these numbers and not others", nor do they explain why some methods call for more participants (e.g. ethnography, ethnoscience, and grounded theory) compared to other approaches (like phenomenology) require less (Mason, 2010).

Unlike what is found in quantitative research, there are no power calculations or quantitative sample size estimation algorithms in qualitative research (Brod, Tesler, & Christensen, 2009). Moreover, based on this review of the literature, there is no consistency among researchers in terms of the suggested sample size parameters that do exist. Thomson (2004) reviewed 50 grounded theory research articles and found sample sizes ranging from 5 to 350. Just over a third (34%) used samples between Creswell's suggested range of 20 to 30 (1998, p. 128), while only 11 studies (or 22%) used samples that conformed to Morse's range of over 30 (1994, p. 225).

Similarly, Mason (2010) concluded that "ten interviews, conducted by an experienced interviewer, will elicit richer data than 50 interviews by an inexperienced or novice researcher. Any of these factors along the qualitative journey can affect how and when saturation is reached and when researchers feel they have enough data". He concluded that "the sample size becomes irrelevant as the quality of data is the measurement of its value". Fundamentally, as suggested by Aldiabat and Le Navenec (2018), "reaching data saturation is a subjective, non-linear, gradual, and unfixed process" (p. 255).

In conclusion, we have assessed the quality of our interview data and determined it to be rich, thick, and strong. Our sample was homogenous in that only highly educated and significantly experienced HR practitioners participated in the study, and the study did not cross disciplines. Based upon a review of the relevant literature cited herein, we have determined that saturation was reached, and that high-quality data was collected during this study. As a result, we have determined that this data serves as a strong and reliable foundation upon which to base our study's findings.

Assessment of the Study's Rigor

Qualitative research does not yield quantitative data, so it does not follow the same rules for testing reliability and validity. This does not mean, though, that qualitative research need not be rigorous in its approach to the evaluation of a study's results. Strauss and Corbin (1990, 1998) provide eight criteria to assess the empirical grounding of a grounded theory study:

1. Are concepts generated?
2. Are the concepts systematically related?
3. Are there many conceptual linkages, and are the categories well developed? Do the categories have conceptual density?
4. Is variation built into the system?
5. Are the conditions under which variations can be found built into the study and explained?
6. Has the process been taken into account?
7. Do the theoretical statements seem significant, and to what extent?
8. Does the theory stand the test of time and become part of the discussions and ideas exchanged among relevant social and professional groups?

At the conclusion of the study, the research findings were evaluated to ensure the empirical grounding of the study according to these criteria. With the exception of whether or not the theory will stand the test of time and become part of future academic conversations (which only time will tell), we have concluded that these criteria were met.

Validity of the Theory

This study resulted in the development of a theory which allows us "to cut through ordinary explanations and understandings and to attend to certain realities and not to others" (Charmaz, 2014, p. 260), so we also tested the validity of the emergent theory. To do this, it was necessary to evaluate the data to ensure that it was "detailed, focused, and full … and that they reveal participants' views, feelings, intentions, and actions as well as the contexts and structures of their lives" given that "researchers generate strong grounded theories with rich data" (Charmaz, p. 23).

Upon completion of this review, it appeared that the new theory and conceptual model was properly supported and grounded in the data which we determined to be both "rich" and plentiful. In addition, a completed grounded theory must meet the following criteria: a close fit with the data, usefulness, and conceptual density, durability over time, modifiability, and explanatory power (e.g. Glaser, 1992; Glaser & Strauss, 1965, 1967). The study's findings were also reviewed to ensure that they were consistent with this reasoning and we answered that question in the affirmative.

Caution About Using These Results

It should be noted that the resulting theory is an interpretation that "depends on the researcher's view; it does not and cannot stand outside of it" (Charmaz, 2014, p. 239). Using this approach gave priority to showing "patterns and connections rather than to linear reasoning" but did not attempt to determine causality (Charmaz, 2006, p. 126).

Rather than contributing verified knowledge, grounded theories seek to offer "plausible explanations" of the data that they have collected (Charmaz, 2006, p. 149). As a result, other researchers may have developed a different understanding of the data. Having said that, we believe that the theory and conceptual model created as a result of this study has made a substantial contribution to both knowledge and practice that will, hopefully, prove to be useful to both HR practitioners and also to their organizations.

Possible Study Limitations

We advise caution when attempting to generalize our findings (or the findings from any qualitative research study) to any other organization. We can only indicate that the data we have is suggestive and representative of a small—but important—group of 26 HR professionals who elected to participate in the study.

Of note, female HR practitioners and those identifying themselves as Caucasian were overrepresented in the present sample. It remains unclear if a more balanced racial profile or if additional male participants would stress alternative aspects of toxin handling or perceive it in a different way; however, we did not identify any inconsistencies in the responses based on gender or racial differences within our existing sample.

While this study does identify the perceptions of the participants as to the systemic variables that may influence the need for toxin handling, based on these findings it is not possible to infer causality. For example, we cannot say with certainty which factors (e.g. restructuring, reductions in force, voluntary retirement programs, mergers and acquisitions) contribute to the most intense level of toxic emotions or which factors increase the level or frequency of toxic emotions at work.

It should also be noted that this study did not result in a purely objective assessment of toxin handling among HR practitioners. Our findings represent the *perceptions* of the HR professionals interviewed for this study. However, perceptions (even inaccurate ones) are important because they affect behavior and a practitioner's sense of well-being, or not. Also unknown is the extent to which these perceptions depended upon the particular organization for which the participant worked and its unique culture.

And finally, as we cautioned previously, other researchers may have interpreted the same data in a different way. Locke (2001, 2002) stresses that a theoretical framework based on a grounded theory approach should simply be regarded as a "theoretical place-marker" in the development of thinking about a complex phenomenon. As a result, the usefulness of the findings should be evaluated based on whether they reveal something substantive about the research topic and can advance our collective knowledge about HR's unique role in the management of toxic emotions in the workplace—which we believe that the study does.

Suggestions for Future Research

Future studies to examine the linkages between emotional intelligence and empathy with toxin handling would be of value. In addition, studies to explore whether expanded training, more organizational communication, the impact of networking with professional colleagues, or formalizing the toxin handling responsibilities by explicitly incorporating them into the job descriptions of HR roles help to reduce levels of toxic workplace emotions would also be of interest. Future research should also investigate how an HR practitioner's personality motivates him or her to engage in toxin handling and how it impacts their ability to cope with its effects.

In addition, it would be useful to examine how other disciplines (e.g. law, accounting, tax, communications) experience toxic workplace emotions and compare and contrast the perceptions of individuals employed within those functions with the perceptions of the HR practitioners who participated in this study. It might also be useful to more closely examine the perceptions of a more balanced sample of participants in terms of both gender and race.

It would also be helpful to explore the differences between HR professionals who burnout and leave the profession and those who exhibit more resilience and find ways to deal with the stress. It would be interesting as well to examine HR practitioners at an earlier stage in their career to examine the effects of toxic emotions on their decision to continue or exit the profession or their organization due to the stressors involved. Moreover, similarities and differences across industries and between for-profit, government, and not-for-profit organizations should be examined.

Another significant contribution would be an examination into which types of workplace situations create the most organizational toxicity and, thus, the need for toxin handling to occur (e.g. restructuring, reductions in force, voluntary retirement programs, mergers and acquisitions). Moreover, understanding how those situations could be managed differently to reduce the organizational toxicity created by them would also be useful.

In addition, the body of literature about emotional labor and HR was identified in the secondary literature review as an area ripe for further study. Combining the issues examined herein to better understand the similarities and differences in the two constructs and how they may overlap would also be useful.

Originality/Value/Implications of the Study

The study resulted in the development of a new grounded theory and conceptual model which suggested that a central aspect of the HR practitioner's role is to act as an organizational toxin handler. This study also confirmed the five core actions of a toxin handler first identified in Frost's (2003, 2004, 2006) ground-breaking work. Further, this empirical study, one of the earliest of its kind to focus on the HR profession, extended Frost's earlier work by finding that coaching and advising managers was an additional core action for toxin handlers working in the HR domain. Finally, the study yielded practical recommendations—both individual and systemic—that may help to minimize the negative impact of toxin handling on HR practitioners while ensuring that this important work can continue to contribute to positive organizational outcomes.

Declaration of No Conflicting Interests

The author(s) declare no potential conflicts of interest with respect to the research, authorship, and/or publication of this article.

Disclaimer

The principal investigator bears the sole responsibility for the study and contents of this final report. The findings reported herein do not necessarily reflect the views of other members of the research team, Sullivan University, the study's participants, or the employees, officers, or directors of the Sullivan University System.

About the Principal Investigator

Teresa A. Daniel, JD, PhD, serves as dean and professor, Human Resource Leadership Programs at Sullivan University (www.sullivan.edu) based in Louisville, KY. She is also the chair for the HRL concentration in the university's PhD in Management program. An active scholar-practitioner, her growing body of research on the problem of workplace bullying, toxic leadership, and sexual harassment has been actively supported by the national Society for Human Resource Management through numerous articles and interviews, as well as by the publication of her most recent book published in 2016 and titled *Stop Bullying at Work: Strategies and Tools for HR, Legal & Risk Management Professionals* (Alexandria, VA: SHRM Books). She has also authored two additional books, plus numerous articles and book chapters, about contemporary issues at the intersection of HR, leadership, employment law, and ethics with a focus on counterproductive workplace behaviors.

About the Research Assistant

Chris Gray is a PhD student in Management with a concentration in HR Leadership at Sullivan University. Gray is also a Human Resources Consultant with the Department of Veterans Affairs. From 2005 to 2009, he proudly served in the US Marine Corps as an infantryman with two tours in Iraq.

Gray's research interests include the employment of veterans, veteran entrepreneurship, and workforce studies.

For Further Information

If you are interested in further discussing the observations and conclusions contained in this report, please contact the Principal Investigator at tdaniel@sullivan.edu.

Acknowledgments

The principal investigator (PI) wishes to acknowledge Chris Gray, a current student in the Sullivan University doctoral program in Management, for his active and enthusiastic involvement in this study. He actively participated in both the participant recruiting and data analysis phases of the project and Gray personally conducted a large number of the interviews. As a result, his contribution to the project was unusually significant and his high-quality work is very much appreciated. I have no doubt that he will be an outstanding scholar-practitioner and he is well on his way.

In addition, the PI wishes to express her sincere appreciation to Sullivan University for the generous faculty research grant which provided funding for the project.

Finally, the PI wishes to express her gratitude to the HR Practitioners (who shall remain anonymous) who generously took the time to be interviewed for this study. Both individually and as a group, they were articulate, thoughtful, smart, and impressive by any measure. Without them, this study would not have been possible and American workplaces would be less humane.

References

Adler, P., & Adler, P. (2012). Expert voices. In S. Baker & R. Edwards (Ed.), *How many qualitative interviews is enough? Expert voices and early career reflections on sampling and cases in qualitative research* (pp. 8–11). Southampton: The National Centre for Research Methods Review Paper.

Aldiabat, K. M., & Le Navenec, C. L. (2018). Data saturation: The mysterious step in grounded theory method. *The Qualitative Report, 23*(1), 245–261.

Bennis, W., & Nanus, B. (1985). *Leaders: The strategies for taking charge.* New York: Harper & Row.

Bertaux, D. (1981). From the life-history approach to the transformation of sociological practice. In D. Bertaux (Ed.), *Biography and society: The life history approach in the social sciences* (pp. 29–45). London: SAGE.

Bonde, D. (2013). *Qualitative market research: When enough is enough.* Retrieved from http://www.raptureconsulting.com/uploads/2/4/3/8/24380515/how_many_qualitative_interviews.pdf.

Brod, M., Tesler, L., & Christensen, T. (2009). Qualitative research and content validity: Developing best practices based on science and experience. *Quality of Life Research, 18*(9), 1263–1278.

Bryant, A. (2002). Re-grounding grounded theory. *Journal of Information Technology: Theory and Application, 4*(1), 25–42.

Bryman, A. (2004). Qualitative research on leadership: A critical but appreciative review. *The Leadership Quarterly, 15*, 729–769.

Charmaz, K. (2003). Grounded theory: Objectivist and constructivist methods. In N. K. Denzin & Y. S. Lincoln (Eds.), *Strategies of qualitative inquiry* (2nd edn., pp. 249–291). London: Sage Publications Limited

Charmaz, K. (2006, 2014). *Constructing grounded theory.* London: Sage Publications Limited.

Conger, J. A. (1998). Qualitative research as the cornerstone methodology for understanding leadership. *The Leadership Quarterly, 9*, 107–121.

Conger, J. A., & Toegel, G. (2002). Action learning and multi-rater feedback as leadership development interventions: Popular but poorly deployed. *Journal of Change Management, 3*(4), 332–348.

Creswell, J. (1998, 2013). *Qualitative inquiry and research design: Choosing among five traditions.* Thousand Oaks, CA: Sage.

Cross, R., Taylor, S., & Zehner, D. (2018, July-August). Collaboration without burnout. *Harvard Business Review.* Retrieved from https://hbr.org/2018/07/collaboration-without-burnout.

Daniel, T. A. (2017, Winter). Managing toxic emotions at work: An examination of HR's unique role as the "organizational shock absorber." *Employment Relations Today, 43*(4), 13–19.

Development Dimensions International. (2016). *High-resolution leadership.* Retrieved from https://www.ddiworld.com/global-offices/united-states/press-room/what-is-the-1-leadership-skill-for-overall-success.

Devi, B. R. (2016, September). A study on human resource perspectives of emotional labour in service sector. *IOSR Journal of Business and Management, 18*(9), 154–158.

Dworkin, S. L. (2012). Sample size policy for qualitative studies using in-depth interviews. *Archives of Sexual Behavior, 41*(6), 1319–1320.

Frost, P. J. (2003). *Toxic emotions at work.* Boston: Harvard Business School Press.

Frost, P. J. (2004). Handling toxic emotions: New challenges for leaders and their organizations. *Organizational Dynamics, 33*(2), 111–127.

Frost, P. J. (2006, March/April). Emotions in the workplace and the important role of toxin handlers. *Ivey Business Journal.* Retrieved from https://iveybusinessjournal.com/publication/emotions-in-the-workplace-and-the-important-role-of-toxin-handlers/.

Frost, P. J., & Robinson, S. (1999, July/August). The toxic handler: Organizational hero—and casualty. *Harvard Business Review, 77*(4), 96–106.

Glaser, B. G. (1992). *Basics of grounded theory analysis.* Mill Valley, CA: The Sociology Press.

Glaser, B. G., & Strauss, A. L. (1965). *Awareness of dying.* Chicago: Aldine.

Glaser, B. G. & Strauss, A. L. (1967). *The discovery of grounded theory: Strategies for qualitative research.* New York, NY: Aldine.

Green, J., & Thorogood, N. (2009, 2004). *Qualitative methods for health research* (2nd edn.). Thousand Oaks, CA: SAGE.

Guest, G., Bunce, A., & Johnson, L. (2006). How many interviews are enough? An experiment with data saturation and variability. *Field Methods, 19*(1), 59–82.

Hennink, M. M., Kaiser, B. N., & Marconi, V. C. (2016). Code saturation versus meaning saturation: How many interviews are enough? *Qualitative Health Research, 27*(4), 1–18.

Hirsch, A. S. (2018, January 15). *Why empathetic HR leaders are more effective.* SHRM resources and tools. Retrieved from https://www.shrm.org/resources andtools/hr-topics/employee-relations/pages/why-empathetic-hr-leaders-are-more-effective.aspx.

Hochschild, A. (1983). *The managed heart: Commercialization of human feeling.* Berkeley: University of California Press.

Jette, D. J., Grover, L., & Keck, C. P. (2003). A qualitative study of clinical decision making in recommending discharge placement from the acute care setting. *Physical Therapy, 83*(3), 224–236.

Kulik, C. T., Cregan, C., Metz, I., & Brown, M. (2009). HR managers as toxin handlers: The buffering effect of formalizing toxin handling responsibilities. *Human Resource Management, 48*(5), 695–716.

Lee, T. W. (1999). *Using qualitative methods in organizational research.* Thousand Oaks, CA: Sage.

Lee, T. W., Mitchell, T. R., & Sablynski, C. J. (1999). Qualitative research in organizational and vocational psychology: 1979–1999. *Journal of Vocational Behavior, 55*,161–187.

Lincoln, Y. S., & Guba, E. G. (1985). *Naturalistic inquiry.* Newbury Park, CA: Sage.

Locke, K. (2001). *Grounded theory in management research.* Thousand Oaks, CA: Sage Publications.

Locke, K. (2002). The grounded theory approach to qualitative research. In F. Drasgow & N. Schmitt (Eds.), *Measuring and analyzing behavior in organizations: Advances in measure and data analysis* (pp. 17–43). San Francisco: Jossey-Bass.

Mason, M. (2010). Sample size and saturation in PhD studies using qualitative interviews. *Qualitative Social Research, 11*(3), Article 8. Retrieved from http://www.qualitative-research.net/index.php/fqs/article/view/1428/3027.

Metz, I., Brown, M., Cregan, C., & Kulik, C. T. (2012). "Toxin handling" and well-being: The case of the human resources manager. *European Journal of Work and Organizational Psychology, 23*(2), 248–262.

Mintzberg, H. (1973). *The nature of managerial work.* New York: Harper & Row

Morse, J. M. (1994). Designing funded qualitative research. In N. K. Denzin & Y. S. Lincoln (Eds.), *Handbook of qualitative research* (2nd edn., pp. 220–235). Thousand Oaks, CA: Sage.

Morse, J. M. (2004). Theoretical saturation. In M. S. Lewis-Beck, A. Bryman, & T. F. Liao (Eds.), *The SAGE encyclopedia of social science research methods* (p. 1123). Thousand Oaks, CA: SAGE.

Morse, J. M. (2015a). "Data were saturated …". *Qualitative Health Research, 25*(5), 587–588.

Morse, J. M. (2015b). Critical analysis of strategies for determining rigor in qualitative inquiry. *Qualitative Health Research, 25*(9), 1212–1222.

O'Brien, E., & Linehan, C. (2014). A balancing act: Emotional challenges in the HR role. *Journal of Management Studies, 51*(8). https://doi: 10.1111/joms.12098.

O'Brien, E., & Linehan, C. (2016, May). The last taboo?: Surfacing and supporting emotional labour in HR work. *The International Journal of Human Resource Management, 29*(4). Retrieved from https://www.tandfonline.com/doi/abs/10.1080/09585192.2016.1184178.

Parry, K. W. (1998). Grounded theory and social process: A new direction for leadership research. *The Leadership Quarterly, 9*(1), 85–105.

Ragin, C. C. (2012). Expert voices, In S. Baker & R. Edwards (Eds.), *How many qualitative interviews is enough? Expert voices and early career reflections on sampling and cases in qualitative research* (p. 34). Southampton: The National Centre for Research Methods Review Paper.

Ritchie, J., Lewis, J., & Elam, G. (2003). Designing and selecting samples. In J. Ritchie & J. Lewis (Eds.), *Qualitative research practice: A guide for social science students and researchers* (pp. 77–108). Thousand Oaks, CA: Sage.

Strauss, A. I., & Corbin, J. (1998, 1990). *Basics of qualitative research: Techniques and procedures for developing grounded theory* (2nd edn.). Thousand Oaks, CA: Sage.

Suddaby, R. (2006). What grounded theory is not. *Academy of Management Journal, 49*, 633–642.

Thomson, B. S. (2004). *Qualitative research: Grounded theory—sample size and validity*. Retrieved from http://www.buseco.monash.edu.au/research/studentdocs/mgt.pdf.

Thomson, S. B. (2011). Sample size and grounded theory. *Journal of Administration and Governance, 5*(1), 45–52.

Van Maanen, J. (1983). Epilogue: Qualitative methods reclaimed. In J. Van Maanen (Ed.), *Qualitative methodology* (pp. 247–268). Thousand Oaks, CA: Sage.

Wargnier, M. (2014). *Emotion regulation responsibilities and psychological well-being: Effects of emotional labour on HR managers and organizations.* INSEAD master's thesis.

Bibliography

American Bar Association. (2012). *Model anti-bullying policy*. Retrieved from http://www.americanbar.org/content/dam/aba/events/labor_law/2012/03/national_conference_on_equal_employment_opportunity_law/mw2012eeo_eisenberg2.authcheckdam.pdf

American Institute of Stress. (n.d.). Retrieved from https://www.stress.org/.

Anderson, C., Brion, S., Moore, D., & Kennedy, J. (2012, October). A status-enhancement account of overconfidence. *Journal of Personality and Social Psychology, 103*(4), 718–735.

Andersson, L. M., & Pearson, C. M. (1999). Tit for tat? The spiraling effect of incivility in the workplace. *Academy of Management Review, 24*, 452–471.

Angyal, A. (1941). *Foundations for a science of personality*. New York: The Commonwealth Fund.

Austen, B. (2012, August). Do you *really* want to be like Steve Jobs? *Wired Magazine*. Retrieved from https://www.cultofmac.com/180287/wireds-new-cover-asks-if-you-really-want-to-be-like-steve-jobs/.

Babiak, P., & Hare, R. D. (2006). *Snakes in suits*. New York: Harper Collins.

Bakker, A. B., LeBlanc, P. M., & Schaufeli, W. B. (2005). Burnout contagion among intensive care nurses. *Journal of Advanced Nursing, 51*, 276–287.

Balfour, A., & Fuller, S. (2010). Why business leaders are profit motivated rather than socially motivated: The role of business education. *The Journal of Global Business Management, 6*(2), 191–197.

Bandura, A. (1973). *Aggression: A social learning analysis*. Englewood Cliffs, NJ: Prentice Hall.

Bass, B. M., & Stogdill, R. M. (1990). *Handbook of leadership: A survey of theory and research*. New York: Free Press.

Bennis, W., & Nanus, B. (1985). *Leaders: The strategies for taking charge*. New York: Harper & Row.
Berglas, S. (1986). *The success syndrome: Hitting bottom when you reach the top*. New York: Plenum Press.
Bertalanffy, L. (1968). *General system theory* (Rev. edn.). New York: George Braziller.
Blake, R. R., & McCanse, A. A. (1991). *Leadership dilemmas: Grid solutions*. Houston, TX: Gulf Publishing Company.
Blake, R. R., & Mouton, J. S. (1964). *The managerial grid*. Houston, TX: Gulf Publishing Company.
Blake, R. R., & Mouton, J. S. (1985). *The managerial grid III*. Houston, TX: Gulf Publishing Company.
Blotnick, S. (1987). *Ambitious men: Their drives, dreams, and delusions*. New York: Viking.
Boddy, C. (1976). *Corporate psychopaths: Organisational destroyers*. New York: Palgrave Macmillan.
Boddy, C. R. (2011). *Corporate psychopaths: Organisational destroyers*. New York: Palgrave Macmillan.
Bowers, D. G., & Seashore, S. E. (1966). Predicting organizational effectiveness with a four-factor theory of leadership. *Administrative Science Quarterly, 11*, 238–263.
Bratis, D., Tselebis, A., Sikaras, C., Moulou, A., Giotakis, K., Zoumakis, E., & Ilias, I. (2009). Alexithymia and its association with burnout, depression and family support among Greek nursing staff. *Human Resources for Health, 7*, 72–75.
Bria, M., Spanu, F., Baban, A., & Dumitrascu, D. L. (2014). Maslach burnout inventory—General survey: Factorial validity and invariance among Romanian healthcare professionals. *Burnout Research, 1*(3), 103–111.
Brodsky, C. (1976). *The harassed worker*. Lexington, MA: Lexington Books.
Bryman, A. (1992). *Charisma and leadership in organizations*. London: Sage.
Bryman, A., Collinson, D., Grint, K., Jackson, G., & Uhl-Bien, M. (Eds.). (2011). *The SAGE handbook of leadership*. London, UK: Sage.
Burns, J. M. (1978). *Leadership*. New York: Harper & Row.
Cappelli, P. (2015, July/August). Why we love to hate HR … and what HR can do about it. *Harvard Business Review*. Retrieved from https://hbr.org/2015/07/why-we-love-to-hate-hr-and-what-hr-can-do-about-it.
Cartwright, D., & Zander, A. (1960). *Group dynamics research and theory*. Evanston, IL: Row, Peterson.
Center for Advanced Human Resource Studies. (2012, February). *Do nice guys—and gals—really finish last? The joint effects of sex and agreeableness on income* (CAHRS Research Link No. 18). Ithaca, NY: Cornell University, ILR School.
Cheng, J. T., Tracy, J. L., Foulsham, T., Kingstone, A., & Henrick, J. (2013). Two ways to the top: Evidence that dominance and prestige are distinct yet viable avenues to social rank and influence. *Journal of Personality & Social Psychology, 104*(1), 103–125.
Ciulla, J. B. (1998). *Ethics: The heart of leadership*. Westport, CT: Praeger.

Ciulla, J. B. (2004). Ethics and leadership effectiveness. In J. Antonakis, A. T. Cianciolo, & R. J. Sternberg (Eds.), *The nature of leadership* (pp. 302–327). Thousand Oaks: Sage Publications.

Collins, J. (2009). *How the mighty fall.* Collins Business Essentials.

Collinson, D. (1988). *Managing the shop floor: Subjectivity, masculinity and workplace culture.* Berlin: Walter de Gruyter & Co..

Conger, J. (1990). The dark side of leadership. *Organizational Dynamics, 19*, 44–55.

Cowan, R. L. (2009). *Walking the tightrope: Workplace bullying and the human resource professional.* Doctoral Dissertation, Texas A & M University.

Crawshaw, L. (2005). *Coaching abrasive executives: Exploring the use of empathy in constructing less destructive interpersonal management strategies.* Doctoral Dissertation, Fielding Graduate University. Retrieved from http://www.bosswhispering.com/Coaching-Abrasive-Executives.pdf.

Crawshaw, L. (2007). *Taming the abrasive manager.* San Francisco, CA: Jossey-Bass.

Daniel, T. A. (2003a). Tools for building a positive employee relations environment. *Employment Relations Today, 30*(2), 51–64. Retrieved from http://onlinelibrary.wiley.com/doi/10.1002/ert.10086/abstract

Daniel, T. A. (2003b). Developing a "culture of compliance" to prevent sexual harassment. *Employment Relations Today, 30*(3), 33–42. Retrieved from http://onlinelibrary.wiley.com/doi/10.1002/ert.10096/abstract

Daniel, T. A. (2006). Bullies in the workplace: A focus on the "abusive disrespect" of employees. *SHRM Whitepapers.* Retrieved from http://moss07.shrm.org/Research/Articles/Articles/Pages/CMS_018341.aspx.

Daniel, T. A. (2009a). *"Tough boss" or workplace bully: A grounded theory study of insights from human resource professionals.* Doctoral Dissertation, Fielding Graduate University. Retrieved from http://gradworks.umi.com/33/50/3350585.html.

Daniel, T. A. (2009b). *Stop bullying at work: Strategies and tools for HR & legal professionals.* Alexandria, VA: SHRM Books. Retrieved from http://shrmstore.shrm.org.

Daniel, T. A. (2009c, July 12–17). Workplace bullying in American organizations: The path from recognition to prohibition. In *53rd Annual Conference of the International Society for the Systems Sciences, The University of Queensland, Brisbane.* Retrieved from http://journals.isss.org/index.php/proceedings53rd/article/viewFile/1209/400.

Daniel, T. A. (2012a, June 13–15). HR in the crossfire: An exploration into the role of HR and workplace bullying. In *8th International Conference on Workplace Bullying and Harassment, University of Copenhagen, Copenhagen, Denmark.* Retrieved from http://bullying2012.com/programme/DETAILED_CONFERENCE_PROGRAMME_version_12.pdf/.

Daniel, T. A. (2012b, Spring). Caught in the crossfire: When HR practitioners become targets of bullying. *Employment Relations Today, 39*(1), 9–16. Retrieved from http://onlinelibrary.wiley.com/doi/10.1002/ert.21349/abstract.

Daniel, T. A. (2012c). LinkedIn Poll: Which of these criticisms of HR create the most conflict between executives and HR professionals? Retrieved from http://

Bibliography

www.linkedin.com/osview/canvas?_ch_page_id=1&_ch_panel_id=1&_ch_app_id=1900&_applicationId=1900&_ownerId=0&appParams=

Daniel, T. A. (2013a, Summer). *Executive success and the increased potential for ethical failure*. SHRM Legal Report. SHRM, Alexandria, VA. Retrieved from http://www.shrm.org/publications/pages/default.aspx.

Daniel, T. A. (2013b). Executive perceptions about the effectiveness of HR. *Employment Relations Today*, 40(2), 1–11.

Daniel, T. A. (2015). *Crossing the line: An examination of toxic leadership in the U.S. Army*. https://doi.org/10.13140/RG.2.1.2700.4969.

Daniel, T. A. (2017a, Winter). Managing toxic emotions at work: An examination of HR's unique role as the "organizational shock absorber". *Employment Relations Today*, 43(4), 13–19.

Daniel, T. A. (2017b). *An examination of exceptional U.S. Army leaders: What they do and how they impact their employees and organization*. https://doi.org/10.13140/RG.2.2.19317.68326.

Daniel, T. A. (2018). *Managing toxic emotions at work: An empirical study of HR's role and its Impact on personal well-being and organizational effectiveness*. https://doi.org/10.13140/RG.2.2.16315.26408.

Daniel, T. A. (2019a, March 6). Viewpoint: HR as toxin handlers. *Society for Human Resource Management HR News*. Retrieved from https://www.shrm.org/resourcesandtools/hr-topics/employee-relations/pages/are-you-a-toxin-handler.aspx.

Daniel, T. A. (2019b, March 13). Viewpoint: How HR can protect itself from toxic emotions. *Society for Human Resource Management HR News*. Retrieved from https://www.shrm.org/resourcesandtools/hr-topics/employee-relations/pages/viewpoint-how-hr-can-protect-itself-from-toxic-emotions.aspx.

Daniel, T. A. (2019c, March 25). Viewpoint: How toxin handlers reduce organizational pain. *Society for Human Resource Management HR News*. Retrieved from https://www.shrm.org/ResourcesAndTools/hr-topics/employee-relations/Pages/Viewpoint-How-Toxin-Handlers-Reduce-Organizational-Pain.aspx.

Daniel, T. A., & Metcalf, G. S. (2001). *The management of people in mergers & acquisitions*. Westport, CT: Quorum Books.

Daniel, T. A., & Metcalf, G. S. (2016). *Stop bullying at work: Strategies and tools for HR, legal & risk management professionals*. Alexandria, VA: SHRM Books.

Davenport, N., Schwartz, R., & Elliot, G. (2005). *Mobbing: Emotional abuse in the American workplace*. Ames, IA: Civil Society Publishing.

Day, D. B., & Antonakis, J. (Eds.). (2012). *The nature of leadership* (2nd ed.). Thousand Oaks, CA: Sage.

De Waal, F. (2009). *The age of empathy: Nature's lessons for a kinder society*. New York: Harmony.

Deming, W. E. (2000). *The new economics for industry, government, education* (2nd ed.). Cambridge: MIT Press.

DiSalvo, D. (2012). *Why jerks get ahead*. Retrieved from http://www.forbes.com/sites/daviddisalvo/2012/08/18/why-jerks-get-ahead/.

Drucker, P. F. (1992). *Managing for the future: The 1990's and beyond.* New York: Penguin Group.
Edwards, D. (1996). *Burning all illusions: A guide to personal and political freedom.* Cambridge, MA: South End Press.
EEOC's *Select Task Force on the Study of Harassment in the Workplace.* (2016). Retrieved from https://www.eeoc.gov/eeoc/task_force/harassment/.
Einarsen, K., Mykletun, R. J., Skogstad, A., Einarsen, S., & Salin, D. (2015, May 24). Ethical infrastructure in combating unethical behavior in organizations: The case of workplace bullying. In *EAWOP Conference, Oslo, Norway.*
Einarsen, S., & Raknes, B. (1997). Harassment in the workplace and the victimization of men. *Violence and Victims, 12*(3), 247–263.
Einarsen, S., Raknes, B., & Matthiesen, S. (1994). Bullying and harassment at work and their relationships to work environment quality: An exploratory study. *European Work & Organizational Psychologist, 4*(4), 381–401.
Einarsen, S., & Salin, D. (2015, May 24). Ethical infrastructure in combating unethical behavior in organizations: The case of workplace bullying. In *EAWOP Conference, Oslo, Norway.*
Einarsen, S., Schanke, M., Aasland, M., & Skogstad, A. (2007). Destructive leadership: A definition and conceptual model. *Leadership Quarterly, 3,* 207–216.
Eisenberger, R., Huntington, R., Hutchison, S., & Sowa, D. (1986). Perceived organizational support. *Journal of Applied Psychology, 71*(3), 500–507.
Figley, C. R. (1982, March). *Traumatization and comfort: Close relationships may be hazardous to your health.* Keynote presentation, Families and Close Relationships: Individuals in social interaction, Texas Tech University. Retrieved from https://www.researchgate.net/publication/282661160_Traumatization_and_comfort_Close_relationships_may_be_hazardous_to_your_health.
Figley, C. R. (Ed.). (1995). *Brunner/Mazel psychological stress series, No. 23. Compassion fatigue: Coping with secondary traumatic stress disorder in those who treat the traumatized.* Philadelphia, PA, US: Brunner/Mazel.
Figley, C. R. (2002). *Treating compassion fatigue.* New York: Brunner-Routledge.
Ford, C. (2005). *Against the grain: An irreverent view of Alberta.* Toronto: McLelland & Stewart Ltd..
Ford, C. (2011, December 11). Bullying won't end until we stop rewarding it. Retrieved from http://beaconnews.ca/blog/2011/12/bullying-won%E2%80%99t-end-until-we-stop-rewarding-it/.
Fox, S., & Cowan, R. L. (2015). Revision of the workplace bullying checklist: The importance of human resource management's role in defining and addressing workplace bullying. *Human Resource Management Journal, 25*(1), 116–130.
Friedman, M. (1970, September 13). The social responsibility of business is to increase its profits. *The New York Times Magazine.* Retrieved from http://www.colorado.edu/studentgroups/libertarians/issues/friedman-soc-resp-business.html.
Frost, P. J. (2003). *Toxic emotions at work.* Boston: Harvard Business School Press.

Frost, P. J. (2004). Handling toxic emotions: New challenges for leaders and their organizations. *Organizational Dynamics, 33*(2), 111–127.

Frost, P. J. (2006, March/April). Emotions in the workplace and the important role of toxin handlers. *Ivey Business Journal*. Retrieved from https://iveybusinessjournal.com/publication/emotions-in-the-workplace-and-the-important-role-of-toxin-handlers/.

Frost, P. J., & Robinson, S. (1999, July/August). The toxic handler: Organizational hero—and casualty. *Harvard Business Review, 77*(4), 96–106.

Furnham, A. (2009). Narcissism at work: The narcissistic personality and organizational relationships. In R. Morrison & S. Wright (Eds.), *Friends and enemies in organizations: A work psychology perspective* (pp. 168–194). New York, NY: Palgrave Macmillan.

Gabriel, Y. (1998). An introduction to the social psychology of insults in organizations. *Human Relations, 5*(11), 1329–1354.

Gardner, J. W. (1990). *On leadership*. New York: Free Press.

Goldsmith, M. (2003). *Global leadership: The next generation*. Upper Saddle River, NJ: Pearson Education, Inc..

Gould, E. (2018). *State of working America wages 2018*. Retrieved from https://www.epi.org/publication/state-of-american-wages-2018/.

Greenleaf, R. K. (1970). *The servant as leader*. Westfield, IN: The Greenleaf Center for Servant Leadership.

Greider, W. (2003). *The soul of capitalism: Opening paths to a moral economy*. New York: Simon & Schuster.

Greider, W. (2009, May 6). The future of the American dream. *The Nation*. Retrieved from http://www.thenation.com/article/future-american-dream.

Greycourt. (2008). *The financial crisis and the collapse of ethical behavior*. Whitepaper No. 44. Pittsburgh, PA: Greycourt & Co.

Gurchiek, K. (2020, February 28). *Is your HR department focused on people or profit?* Society for Human Resource Management. Retrieved from https://www.shrm.org/resourcesandtools/hr-topics/organizational-and-employee-development/pages/is-hrs-focus-on-the-people-or-the-business.aspx

Hammonds, K. H. (2005, August 1). Why we hate HR. *Fast Company*. Retrieved from https://www.fastcompany.com/53319/why-we-hate-hr

Hare, R. D. (1993). *Without conscience: The disturbing world of psychopaths among us*. New York: The Guilford Press.

Hartling, L., & Sparks, E. (2002). *Relational-cultural practice: Working in a non-relational world*. No. 97. Wellesley, MA: Stone Center Working Papers Series.

Healthy Workplace Bill. Retrieved from http://www.healthyworkplacebill.org.

Hearn, J., & Parkin, W. (2001). *Gender, sexuality and violence in organizations*. London: Sage.

Hemphill, J. K., & Coons, A. E. (1957). Development of the leader behavior description questionnaire. In R. M. Stogdill & A. E. Coons (Eds.), *Leader behavior: Its description and measurement* (Research Monograph No. 99). Columbus: Ohio State University, Bureau of Business Research.

Hersh, S. M. (2004, May 10). Torture at Abu Ghraib. *The New Yorker*. Retrieved from http://www.newyorker.com/archive/2004/05/10/040510fa_fact.

Hickman, G. R. (Ed.). (2009). *Leading organizations: Perspectives for a new era* (2nd ed.). Thousand Oaks, CA: Sage.

Hoel, H., & Cooper, C. (2000). *Destructive conflict and bullying at work*. Manchester UK: University of Manchester Institute of Science and Technology.

Hoel, H., & Salin, D. (2003). Organizational antecedents of workplace bullying. In S. Einarsen, H. Hoel, D. Zapf, & C. Cooper (Eds.), *Bullying and emotional abuse in the workplace: International perspectives in research and practice*. London: Taylor & Francis.

Hoffman, R., Casnocha, B., & Yeh, C. (2013, May 23). Tours of duty: The new employer-employee compact. *Harvard Business Review*. Retrieved from http://hbr.org/2013/06/tours-of-duty-the-new-employer-employee-compact/ar/1.

Horn, S. (2002). *Take the bully by the horns: Stop unethical, uncooperative, or unpleasant people from running and ruining your life*. New York: St. Martin's Griffin.

Hornstein, H. A. (1996). *Brutal bosses and their prey: How to identify and overcome abuse in the workplace*. New York: Riverhead Books.

Hornstein, H. A. (2003, November/December). Workplace incivility: An unavoidable product of human nature and organizational nurturing. *Ivey Business Journal, 68*, 1–7.

Huffington, A. (2013). *Smith College 2013 Commencement Speech*. Retrieved from https://www.smith.edu/about-smith/smith-history/smith-commencement-speakers/college-events-commencement-speech-2013.

Internet Engineering Task Force. Retrieved from http://www.ietf.org/.

Ireland, J. L. (2000). 'Bullying' among prisoners: A review of research. *Aggression and Violent Behavior, 5*(2), 201–215.

Janove, J. (2011, August). Become a compliance coach. *HR Magazine, 56*(8). Retrieved from http://www.shrm.org/Publications/hrmagazine/EditorialContent/2011/0811/Pages/0811legal.aspx.

Johns, N., & Menzel, P. J. (1999). 'If you can't stand the heat!'... kitchen violence and culinary art. *Hospitality Management, 18*, 99–109.

Kaplan, R. (1991). *Beyond ambition*. San Francisco, CA: Jossey-Bass.

Katz, D., & Kahn, R. L. (1951). Human organization and worker motivation. In L. R. Tripp (Ed.), *Industrial productivity* (pp. 146–171). Madison, WI: Industrial Relations Research Association.

Katz, R. L. (1955). Skills of an effective administrator. *Harvard Business Review, 33*(1), 33–42.

Kelly, C. M. (1988). *The destructive achiever*. Reading, MA: Addison-Wesley.

Kets de Vries, M. F. (1989). Leaders who self-destruct: The causes and cures. *Organizational Dynamics, 17*, 5–17.

Kirkpatrick, S. A., & Locke, E. A. (1991). Leadership: Do traits matter? *The Executive, 5*, 48–60.

Kochan, T., & Shulman, B. (2007, February 22). A new social contract: Restoring dignity and balance to the economy. Briefing Paper #184. Retrieved from www.epi.org.

Krakel, M. (1997). Rent-seeking in organisationen- eine okonomishe analyse sozial schadlichen verhaltens. *Schmalenbachs Zeitschrift fur Betriebswirtschaftliche Forschung, 49*(6), 535–555.

Kramer, R. M. (2006). The great intimidators. *Harvard Business Review*. Retrieved from http://hbr.org/2006/02/the-great-intimidators/ar/1.

Kulik, C. T., Cregan, C., Metz, I., & Brown, M. (2009). HR managers as toxin handlers: The buffering effect of formalizing toxin handling responsibilities. *Human Resource Management, 48*(5), 695–716.

LaBier, D. (1986). *Modern madness: The emotional fallout of success*. Reading, MA: Addison-Wesley.

Lee, D. (2000). An analysis of workplace bullying in the UK. *Personnel Review, 29*(5), 593–610.

Levering, R. (1988). *A great place to work: What makes some employers so good-and most so bad*. New York: Random House.

Levinson, H. (1978, May-June). The abrasive personality. *Harvard Business Review, 56*, 86–94.

Lewin, K., Lippitt, R., & White, R. (1939). Patterns of aggressive behaviour in experimentally created social climates. *Journal of Social Psychology, 10*, 271–299.

Lewin, K., Lippitt, R., & White, R. (1939). Patterns of aggressive behaviour in experimentally created social climates. *Journal of Social Psychology, 10*, 271–299.

Leymann, H. (1990). Mobbing and psychological terror at workplaces. *Violence and Victims, 52*, 119–126.

Leymann, H. (1996). The content and development of mobbing at work. *European Journal of Work and Organizational Psychology, 5*(2), 165–184.

Likert, R. (1961). *New patterns of management*. New York: McGraw-Hill.

Likert, R. (1967). *The human organization: Its management and value*. New York: McGraw-Hill.

Livingston, R. W. S. (2001). *Bias in the absence of malice: The phenomenon of unintentional discrimination*. Unpublished doctoral dissertation, The Ohio State University.

Lord, R. G., DeVader, C. L., & Alliger, G. M. (1986). A meta-analysis of the relationship between personality traits and leadership perceptions: An application of validity generalization procedures. *Journal of Applied Psychology, 71*, 402–410.

Lubit, R. (2004). *Coping with toxic managers, subordinates… and other difficult people*. Upper Saddle River, NJ: Financial Times Press.

Ludeman, K., & Erlandson, E. (2006). *Alpha male syndrome*. Boston, MA: Harvard Business School Press.

Ludwig, D. C., & Longenecker, C. O. (1993). The "Bathsheba syndrome": The ethical failure of successful leaders. *Journal of Business Ethics, 12*, 265–273.

Maccoby, M. (2003). *The productive narcissist: The promise and peril of visionary leadership*. New York: Broadway Books.

Magee, J. C., & Langner, C. A. (2008). How personalized and socialized power motivation facilitate antisocial and prosocial decision-making. *Journal of Research in Personality, 42*, 1547–1559.

Makower, J. (2006, November 24). Milton Friedman and the social responsibility of business. Retrieved from http://www.greenbiz.com/news/2006/11/24/milton-friedman-and-social-responsibility-business

Mann, R. D. (1959). A review of the relationship between personality and performance in small groups. *Psychological Bulletin, 56*, 241–270.

Martin, C. (2016). *The new American dream*. TED Talk. Retrieved from https://www.ted.com/talks/courtney_e_martin_the_new_american_dream?language=en

Maslach, C., & Goldberg, J. (1998). Prevention of burnout: New perspectives. *Applied and Preventive Psychology, 7*, 63–74. https://doi.org/10.1016/S0962-1849(98)80022-X

Maslach, C., & Leiter, M. P. (1997). *The truth about burnout: How organizations cause personal stress and what to do about it*. San Francisco: Jossey-Bass.

Maslow, A. H. (1943). A theory of human motivation. *Psychological Review, 50*(4), 370–396. Retrieved from http://psychclassica.yorku.ca/Maslow/motivation.htm

McCarthy, N. (2019, September 18). The number of uninsured Americans is rising again—And young adults are most likely to lack coverage. *Forbes*. Retrieved from https://www.forbes.com/sites/niallmccarthy/2019/09/18/the-number-of-uninsured-americans-is-rising-again%2D%2Dand-young-adults-who-are-most-likely-to-lack-coverage/#2fc251795b62.

McClelland, D. C. (1975). *Power: The inner experience*. NY: Irvington.

McIntosh, G. L., & Rima, S. D. (1997). *Overcoming the dark side of leadership: The paradox of personal dysfunction*. Grand Rapids, MI: Baker Books.

McIntosh, G. L., & Rima, S. D. (1997). *Overcoming the dark side of leadership: The paradox of personal dysfunction*. Grand Rapids, MI: Baker Books.

Meadows, D. (1999). *Leverage points: Places to intervene in a system*. The Sustainability Institute. Retrieved from http://www.sustainer.org/pubs/Leverage_Points.pdf.

Meadows, D. (2008). *Thinking in systems: A primer*. White River Junction, VT: Chelsea Green Publishing.

Miller, J. B. (1986). *What do we mean by relationships?* The Stone Center for Development Services & Studies at Wellesley College Colloquium 1(2).

Mirza, B. (2011). *Company leaders tell HR: Know the business and be relevant*. Retrieved from http://www.shrm.org/hrdisciplines/businessleadership/articles/Pages/BeRelevant.aspx.

Moore, C., Detert, J. R., Klebe Trevino, L., Baker, V. L., & Mayer, D. M. (2012). Why employees do bad things: Moral disengagement and unethical organizational behavior. *Personnel Psychology, 65*, 1–48.

Moss, J. (2020, February 21). Viewpoint: Rethinking workplace burnout. *Society for Human Resources Management's HR Daily*. Retrieved from https://www.shrm.org/

ResourcesAndTools/hr-topics/employee-relations/Pages/Viewpoint-Rethinking-Workplace-Burnout.aspx.

Mumford, M. D. (2006). *Pathways to outstanding leadership: A comparative analysis of charismatic, ideological, and pragmatic leaders*. Mahway, NJ: Lawrence Erlbaum.

Mumford, M. D., Zaccaro, S. J., Harding, F. D., Jacobs, T. O., & Fleishman, E. A. (2000). Leadership skills for a changing world: Solving complex social problems. *Leadership Quarterly, 11*(1), 11–35.

Mundy, J. C. (2012, July 5). Why HR still isn't a strategic partner. *Harvard Business Review*. Retrieved from http://blogs.hbr.org/cs/2012/07/why_hr_still_isnt_a_strategic_partner.html.

Namie, G., & Namie, R. F. (2000, 2003, 2009). *The bully at work: What you can do to stop the hurt and reclaim your dignity on the job*. Naperville, IL: Sourcebooks.

Neuman, J., & Baron, R. (2011). Social antecedents of bullying: A social interactionist perspective. In S. Einarsen, H. Hoel, D. Zapf, & C. Cooper (Eds.), *Bullying and harassment in the workplace: Developments in theory, research, and practice* (pp. 149–174). New York, NY: CRC Press.

Nielsen, R. P. (1987). What can managers do about unethical management? *Journal of Business Ethics, 4*, 65–70.

Northouse, P. G. (2013). *Leadership: Theory and practice* (6th ed.). Thousand Oaks, CA: Sage.

Nunberg, G. (2012a, August 15). Why do we idolize jerks? Retrieved from http://www.alternet.org/culture/why-do-we-idolize-jerks.

Nunberg, G. (2012b). *Ascent of the A-word: Assholism, the first sixty years*. New York: Public Affairs/Perseus Books.

O'Leary-Kelly, A. M., Griffin, R. W., & Glew, D. J. (1996). Organization-motivated aggression: A research framework. *Academy of Management Review, 21*(1), 225–253.

O'Moore, M. (2000). *Summary report on the national survey on workplace bullying in Ireland*. Dublin: The Anti-Bullying Research Centre, Trinity College.

Patton, C. (2020, February 17). What's keeping HR up at night in 2020? *Human Resource Executive*. Retrieved from https://hrexecutive.com/whats-keeping-hr-up-at-night-in-2020/

Pearson, C., & Porath, C. (2009). *The cost of bad behavior*. New York, NY: Penguin Books.

Peck, M. S. (1998). *People of the lie: The hope for healing human evil*. New York: Touchtone.

Peele, S. (2011, April 28). Bullying works: Why people fear Donald Trump. *Psychology Today*. Retrieved from http://www.psychologytoday.com/blog/addiction-in-society/201104/bullying-works-why-people-fear-donald-trump.

Peters, T. J., & Waterman, R. H. (1982). *In search of excellence: Lessons from America's best-run companies*. New York: Harper Collins.

Pinchot, G. (Online). *Brainy quotes*. Retrieved from https://www.brainyquote.com/quotes/gifford_pinchot_140386.

Pirsig, R. (1974). *Zen and the art of motorcycle maintenance.* New York: Harper Torch.
Portnoy, D. (2011, July/August). Burnout and compassion fatigue: Watch for the signs. *Health Progress, 92*, 46–50.
Potter, P., Deschields, T., Divanbeigi, J., Berger, J., Cipriano, D., Norris, L., & Olsen, S. (2010, October 14). Compassion fatigue and burnout: Prevalence among oncology nurses. *Clinical Journal of Oncology Nursing, 5*, 56–62.
Price, T. L. (2000). Explaining ethical failures of leadership. *The Leadership & Organization Development Journal, 12*, 177–184.
Price, T. L. (2006). *Understanding ethical failures in leadership.* Cambridge, MA: Cambridge University Press.
Protess, B. (2012, August 14). Wells Fargo settles mortgage investments case for $6.5 million. *New York Times.* Retrieved from http://dealbook.nytimes.com/2012/08/14/wells-fargo-settles-mortgage-investments-case-for-6-5-million/
Rogers, K. (2011, November 3). Why being the office jerk could pay off. Retrieved from http://www.foxbusiness.com/personal-finance/2011/11/03/workplace-jerks-make-more-money/#ixzz2NMghSBqR.
Rost, J. C. (1991). *Leadership for the twenty-first century.* New York: Praeger.
Salin, D. (2003). Ways of explaining workplace bullying: A review of enabling, motivating, and precipitating structures and processes in the work environment. *Human Relations, 56*(10), 1213–1232.
Schaufeli, W. B., & Enzmann, D. (1998). *The burnout companion to study and practice: A critical analysis.* London: Taylor & Francis.
Schouten, R., & Silver, J. (2012). *Almost a psychopath: Do I (or does someone I know) have a problem with manipulation and lack of empathy?* Center City, MN: Hazelden.
Scott, W. R., & Davis, G. F. (2007). *Organizations and organizing: Rational, natural and open system perspectives.* Upper Saddle River, N.J.: Pearson.
Senge, P. M. (1990). *The fifth discipline: The art and practice of the learning organization.* New York: Doubleday.
Sewell, G., & Wilkinson, B. (1992). Empowerment or emasculation? Shop floor surveillance in a total quality organization. In P. Blyton & P. Turnbull (Eds.), *Reassessing human resource management.* London: SAGE.
Silver-Greenburg, J., & Craig, S. (2012, August 14). JP Morgan trading loss may exceed $9 billion. *The New York Times.* Retrieved from http://dealbook.nytimes.com/2012/06/28/jpmorgan-trading-loss-may-reach-9-billion/
Society for Human Resource Management. (2009). *SHRM ranks leadership qualities for HR professionals.* Retrieved from www.shrm.org/about/pressroom/PressReleases/Pages/SHRMRanksLeadershipQualities.aspx.
Society for Human Resource Management. (2012a). *SHRM survey findings: Workplace bullying.* Retrieved from http://www.shrm.org/Research/SurveyFindings/Articles/Pages/WorkplaceBullying.aspx

Bibliography

Society for Human Resource Management. (2013, May). *Workplace forecast*. Retrieved from https://www.shrm.org/ResourcesAndTools/hr-topics/behavioral-competencies/Documents/13-0146%20workplace_forecast_full_fnl.pdf.

Society for Human Resource Management. (2016a). *The SHRM body of competency and knowledge*. Retrieved from https://www.shrm.org/Documents/SHRM-BoCK-FINAL.pdf.

Society for Human Resource Management. (2016b). *Employee satisfaction and engagement: Revitalizing a changing workforce*. Retrieved from https://www.shrm.org/Research/SurveyFindings/Articles/Documents/2016-Employee-Job-Satisfaction-and-Engagement-Report.pdf.

Society for Human Resource Management. (n.d.). *SHRM competency model*. Retrieved from https://www.shrm.org/learningandcareer/career/pages/shrm-competency-model.aspx.

Society for Human Resource Management Foundation. (2016c). *Creating a more human workplace where employees and businesses thrive*. Retrieved from https://www.shrm.org/about/foundation/products/documents/4-16%20human%20workplace-final.pdf.

Sperry, L. (2009). Mobbing and bullying: A consulting psychology perspective and overview. *Consulting Psychology Journal, 61*(3), 190–201.

Stogdill, R. M. (1948). Personal factors associated with leadership: A survey of the literature. *Journal of Psychology, 25*, 35–71.

Stogdill, R. M. (1974). *Handbook of leadership: A survey of theory and research*. New York: Free Press.

Summers, C. W. (2000). Employment at will in the United States: The divine right of employers. *University of Pennsylvania Journal of Labor & Employment Law, 3*(65), 67–68.

Sutton, R. I. (2007). *The no asshole rule: Building a civilized workplace and surviving one that isn't*. New York: Warner Business Books.

Tangel, A. (2012, August 14). Standard Chartered to pay $340 million in money-laundering case. *Los Angeles Times*. Retrieved from http://www.latimes.com/business/money/la-fi-mo-standard-chartered-settles-new-york-case-20120814,0,6816539.story

Thorbecke, C. (2020, January 10). The Dow Jones reaches 29,000 for the 1st time in history. *ABC News*. Retrieved from https://abcnews.go.com/Business/dow-jones-broke-29000-1st-time-history/story?id=68195223

Thylefors, I. (1987). *Scapegoats: On expulsion and bullying in working life*. Stockholm: Naturoch Kultur.

Treadway, D. C., Shaughnessy, B. A., Breland, J. W., Yang, J., & Reeves, M. (2013). Political skill and the job performance of bullies. *Journal of Managerial Psychology, 28*(3), 273–289.

Ulrich, D. (1998). *Measuring human resources: An overview of practice and a prescription for results.* Retrieved from https://doi.org/10.1002/(SICI)1099-050X(199723)36:3<303::AID-HRM3>3.0.CO;2-%23.

Ulrich, D. (2007). *Human resource champions: The next agenda for adding value and delivering results.* Boston: Harvard Business School Press.

Van Rooy, D. L., & Oehler, K. (2013). *The evolution of employee opinion surveys: The voice of employees as a strategic management tool.* SHRM-SIOP Science of HR White Paper Series. Retrieved from https://www.shrm.org/Research/Articles/Documents/SIOP%20-%20Employee%20Engagement%20final.pdf

VanKleef, M., Homan, G. A., Finkenauer, A. C., Gundemir, S., & Stamkon, E. (2011). Breaking the rules to rise to power: How norm violators gain power in the eyes of others. *Social Psychological and Personality Science, 2*(5), 500–507.

Vartia, M. (1996). The sources of bullying: Psychological work environment and organizational climate. *European Journal of Work & Organizational Psychology, 5*(2), 203–214.

Weaver, C., & Mathews, A.W. (2013, May 20). Employers eye bare-bones health plans under new law. *The Wall Street Journal.* Retrieved from http://online.wsj.com/article/SB10001424127887324787004578493274030598186.html.

Wigert, B., & Agrawal, S. (2018, July 12). Employee burnout, Part 1: The 5 main causes. *Gallup.* Retrieved from https://www.gallup.com/workplace/237059/employee-burnout-part-main-causes.aspx.

Wikipedia. (n.d.). *Perceived organizational support.* Retrieved from https://en.wikipedia.org/wiki/Perceived_organizational_support.

Workplace Bullying Institute U.S. Workplace Bullying Survey. (2007). Retrieved from http://www.workplacebullying.org/wbiresearch/wbi-2007/.

Workplace Bullying Institute U.S. Workplace Bullying Survey. (2010). Retrieved from http://workplacebullying.org/multi/pdf/WBI_2010_Natl_Survey.pdf.

World Health Organization. (2019, May 28). *Burn-out an "occupational phenomenon": International classification of diseases.* Retrieved from https://www.who.int/mental_health/evidence/burn-out/en/

Yamada, D. C. (2008). Workplace bullying and ethical leadership. *Journal of Values-Based Leadership, 1*(2). Retrieved from http://papers.ssrn.com/sol3/papers.cfm?abstract_id=1301554.

Yamada, D. C. (2013a, March 1). Emerging American legal responses to workplace bullying. *Temple Political & Civil Rights Law Review, 22,* Suffolk University Law School Research Paper No. 13-7. Retrieved from http://ssrn.com/abstract=2242945.

Yamada, D. C. (2013b, April 1). Words rarely heard: 'Boss, I think you need to get some help'. *Minding the Workplace Blog.* Retrieved from http://newworkplace.wordpress.com/2013/04/page/2/.

Zaccaro, S. J., Kemp, C., & Bader, P. (2004). Leader traits and attributes. In J. Antonakis, A. T. Cianciolo, & R. J. Sternberg (Eds.), *The nature of leadership* (pp. 101–124). Thousand Oaks, CA: Sage.

Zapf, D., & Einarsen, S. (2011). Individual antecedents of bullying: Victims and perpetrators. In S. Einarsen, H. Hoel, D. Zapf, & C. Cooper (Eds.), *Bullying and harassment in the workplace: Developments in theory, research and practice* (pp. 177–200). New York, NY: CRC Press.

Zapf, D., & Warth, K. (1997). Bullying: Warfare in the workplace. *Psychologie Heute, 24*(8), 20–24, 28–29.

Zimbardo, P. (2008). *The Lucifer effect: Understanding how good people turn evil.* New York: Random House Trade Paperbacks.

Index

NUMBERS AND SYMBOLS
#Coronavirus, 1
#Coronavirus pandemic, 13

A
Abrasive personality, 18
Abu Ghraib prison, 30
Abusive conduct, 23
Abusive leaders, 21
Achievement of high
 standards, 122–123
Advise and coach managers, 51
Alpha males, 19
Alpha risks, 19
American Institute of Stress, 84
Anger, 75
Angyal, Andras, 29
Anxiety, 59
Armstrong, Lance, 37
"At will" employment, 11
Audit key processes, 106

B
Bad behavior, 21
Bad news, 56

Beautiful struggle, 135
Bertalanffy, Ludwig von, 29
Boundaries, 114–115
Burnout, 75, 79–85
Burns, J.M., 119
Business knowledge, 69
Busyness, 133

C
Calling, 79
Celebrities, 37
Charisma of villainy, 21
Checks and balances, 42
Chronic toxicity, 59
Civility, 30
Claims of discrimination and
 harassment, 60
Climate surveys, 106–107
Clinton, Bill (President), 37
Coaching and training, 69
Communication, 69
Community of support, 115
Compassion fatigue, 79–85
Cooperation, 29
Coronavirus Aid, Relief, and Economic
 Security Act, 13

"Cost of caring", 80
"Culture of care", 102
Culture of respect, 105

D
Daniel, T.A., 56
"The dark side of leadership", 41
De-escalate emotional situations, 60
Develop their people, 121
DeWaal, Francis, 28
Dignity at work, 12
Division of labor, 29
"DNA" of organizations, 26
Dominance, 20
Dual roles, 55

E
Edwards, John, 37
EEOC, 106
Efficiency, 10
Emotional exhaustion, 75, 77
Emotional intelligence, 121
Emotionally expansive, 39
Empathetic listening, 51
Empathy, 30
Employee Assistance Program (EAP), 115
Employee morale, 59
Employee well-being, 3
Employment relationship, 10
The "Emptiness Syndrome", 40
Ethical dilemmas, 41
Ethical drivers, 37–42
Evil personality, 19
Exceptional leaders, 121–124
Expand employee communications, 103
Expansive executive, 18

F
Families First Coronavirus Response Act, 13
Fear, 59
Fixers, 3
Flow, 97
Focus on excellence, 23
Formalize toxin handling responsibilities, 101–102
Friction, 97
Frost, P.J., 56

G
Gallup organization, 82
"Golden boy" syndrome, 19
Good leaders, 121
Great intimidators, 18
Guard rails, 37

H
Hammonds, K.H., 66
Hazing, 23
Heart attacks, 76
Heightened fear of failure, 39
Highly personalized caring, 123
HR leadership, 69
Huffington, A., 134
Humane, 12
Humor, 24

I
The immune system, 1
Increased health costs, 59
Inflated ego, 40
Innate personality characteristics, 45–46
Insults, 25

Intentional partnership, 102
Internal police, 70
Internet Engineering Task Force (IETF), 29

J

Jerk, 21
Jobs, Steve, 21, 40

K

Kindness, 30

L

Labor unions, 10
Lack of balance, 39
Lack of sleep, 75
Laissez-faire style of leadership, 23
Lawsuits, 60
Leadership research, 119
Lead with tomorrow in mind, 121
Low perceived risk, 22–24

M

Macro strategies, 101–110
Malice, 19
Management prerogative, 11
Martin, C., 135
Maslach Burnout Inventory, 84
Maximization of profits, 8–9
Metrics, 106
Micro-political behavior, 24
Micro strategies, 113–116
Mission accomplishment, 121
Modeling and imitation, 23
More litigation, 59
Morgan, JP, 42

N

Natural order, 28
Natural systems, 26
No consequences, 22–24

O

On jokes and banter, 24
On Results, 18–19
Open systems, 26
Organizational culture, 23
Organizational effectiveness, 3
Organizational "guard rails", 42
Organizational pain, 51–56
"Organizational shock absorbers", 48
Organizational strategies, 101–110
Organizational systems, 31
Organizational toxicity, 1, 7
Organizational toxin handler, 2, 3

P

Paradox of success, 37, 42
Parent-child relationship, 9
Pecking order, 25
Perceived organizational support, 105
Personal autonomy, 42
Personal excellence, 122–123
Personal risk, 73
Personnel work by other means, 25
Physical exhaustion, 75
Pinchot, G., 99
Positive self-worth, 49
Power, 22
Prestige, 20
Privileged access, 38–39
Productivity, 59
Professional credibility, 69
Professionalism, 49
Profitability, 59

Psychologically healthy workplace, 131
Purpose, 49

R

Ranking of employees, 25
Rational systems, 26
Recognize and appreciate the work, 104
Reframe difficult messages, 51
Regard for others, 135
Regard for self, 135
Regard for society, 135
Rent-seeking behavior, 24
Respect and civility at work, 106
Respectful, 12
Results at all costs, 20
Reward system, 25
Robinson, S., 56
Rotate HR practitioners, 103
Rudeness, 22

S

Sadness, 75
"Seat at the table", 99
Select Task Force on the Study of Harassment in the Workplace, 106
Self-care, 113–114
Self-efficacy, 49
Sense of exemption from rules, 40
Sense of meaning, 49
SHRM, 110
Smith College, 134
Social contract, 9, 10
Socialized power, 120
Societal disconnect, 11
Soft skills training, 103–104
Spencer, Herbert, 28
Standard Chartered, 42
Stanford Prison Experiment (SPE), 30
Strategic business partner/compliance coach, 70
Strategic communication, 51

Strategic partner, 69
Strengths of HR professionals, 91
Stress, 39, 75, 77
Strokes, 76
Strong management, 21

T

TED, 135
Tough bosses, 19, 122
"Tour of duty", 108
Toxic, 1
Toxic workplace, 7
Toxikon, 1
Toxin handlers, 1
Toxin handling role, 75
Trump, Donald, 21
Trust, 103
Turnover, 59

U

"The undisciplined pursuit of more", 39
Use of power, 120–121

W

Wall Street, 41
Weak leaders, 23
Weaknesses of HR professionals, 91–92
Well-being, 76
Wells Fargo Bank, 42
Woods, Tiger, 37
Work-life balance, 115–116
Workplace bullies, 19
World Health Organization (WHO), 82

Z

Zimbardo, Philip, 30

Printed in the United States
By Bookmasters